WTF?
AMERICA

How to Survive 101 of the Worst
F*#!-ing Situations in the United States

Gregory Bergman and Jodi Miller

Adamsmedia
Avon, Massachusetts

Published by Adams Media,
a division of F+W Media, Inc.
57 Littlefield Street, Avon, MA 02322. U.S.A.
www.adamsmedia.com

ISBN 10: 1-4405-4111-6
ISBN 13: 978-1-4405-4111-7
eISBN 10: 1-4405-4254-6
eISBN 13: 978-1-4405-4254-1

Printed in the United States of America.

10   9   8   7   6   5   4   3   2   1

Many of the designations used by manufacturers and sellers to distinguish their product are claimed as trademarks. Where those designations appear in this book and Adams Media was aware of a trademark claim, the designations have been printed with initial capital letters.

Certain sections of this book deal with activities that would be in violation of various federal, state, and local laws if actually carried out. We do not advocate the breaking of any law. The authors, Adams Media, and F+W Media, Inc. do not accept liability for any injury, loss, legal consequence, or incidental or consequential damage incurred by reliance on the information or advice provided in this book. The information in this book is for entertainment purposes only.

This book is available at quantity discounts for bulk purchases.
For information, please call 1-800-289-0963.

contents

Introduction

America is the greatest nation that has and will ever exist on Earth. It's the land of the free. The home of the brave. And the only place where you can regularly find an affordable cheeseburger the size of a dwarf's head. America is so star-spangled awesome that everyone on Earth is envious of and affronted by our freedom. Take the freedom to own guns, for instance. Nowhere else in the world can you carry a concealed handgun into a shopping mall without a permit. Now that's freedom! Not to mention that having a handgun makes for a great negotiating tool when haggling over prices.

Yep, the USA is the pride of nations, a bastion of freedom in a world of socialist "democracies" that use their resources to do inane things like provide basic health care for their citizens. But not here. Here in America

you've got to pull yourself up by your bootstraps and take charge of your destiny. And if you can't afford boots—well, then too fucking bad!

But America isn't perfect. True, it's damn close, but there are still some situations in these great fifty states that can trip you up, situations that make you say "WTF?" Some WTF? Situations are unique to a specific region, like finding out that the girl you took home in San Francisco wasn't no girl, and then there are ones that are unique to the nation as a whole, like getting sick without health insurance. But have no fear. WTF? is here to help you navigate 101 of the worst F*#!-ing situations in America. All you have to do now, you illiterate American fool, is turn the damn page.

ART CREDITS

the state of america today

1. You get sick and you don't have health insurance.

Hey, who needs health insurance, right? It's not like you are going to get hit by a bus tomorrow or something. Health insurance is for European socialist pussies, not for real Americans like you. Real cowboys just suck the venom out of a snake bite, and you don't need no doctor for that. But, turns out that you aren't invincible after all. Yeah, remember those headaches and the ringing in your ear that you thought was nothing? Well, you were right if by "nothing" you meant a fucking brain tumor. Ahhh!!!! WTF?

The WTF Approach to Getting Sick in America

➤ OPTION #1

Stop whining and pull yourself up by your bootstraps. Hey, this isn't France, okay? We believe in individual responsibility. It's not the tax payer's fault that you got some rare brain disease, it's your fault. Take some responsibility, put your brain (before it deteriorates and kills you) to good use, and get rich. Now enjoy the best health care in the world. Because America does have the best health care—for millionaires. For everyone else it sucks balls.

➤ OPTION #2

Move to Massachusetts. There are a few states whose laws express this crazy idea that having health care is a basic right of citizenship, not an expensive privilege. LOL. Friggin' pinko commies!

➤ OPTION #3

Become a Christian Scientist. The Church of Christian Science isn't really a fan of science. Fanatical Christian Scientists don't believe in health care. Instead, they believe that prayer is the best way to cure diseases. It's also the cheapest. So don't fret that you can't talk to a doctor; talk to Jesus instead. He'll fix you right up. And, if he doesn't, you will go to a better place anyhow. You can't lose!

➤ OPTION #4

Play gay. It's a fact that while some states don't recognize same-sex marriage almost every state does allow gay people to be on their partner's health care plan. Ask one of your buddies to help you out and pretend to be gay, just until you get back on your feet financially or you get a job that has benefits. Then you can come out of the straight closet.

HEALTH CARE TIPS

Since you might be one of the millions of Americans without health care coverage who can't afford to see a doctor, here are some basic health tips.

- Prevention. Many illnesses Americans suffer from are preventable, like type 2 diabetes. This means less freedom fries and more time in spin class.
- Smoking. Really not a good idea. One of five deaths is smoking related.
- Don't become a pop star. Michael Jackson, Whitney Houston, Amy Winehouse. Hmm. Looks like we should add "Don't do drugs" to this list.

2. You're in the Occupy movement but love taking showers.

You've always believed in fighting the good fight, so when the Occupy movement came around you were right on the front lines. This is something you feel is very important—plus there are super-hot liberal girls there. But you soon realize this might not be for you. People are sleeping outside in tents. In the rain! There are no showers, no bathrooms, nothing. You want to help the cause, but you don't want to live like an animal while doing it. WTF?

The WTF Approach to Staying Clean While Protesting

➤ OPTION #1

Go home. Look, no one says you have to be there 24/7. Sure, the real die-hard protesters are camping out, but that doesn't mean you have to. Blog about the cause from the comfort of your own home. Eat Chinese food, watch *The Jersey Shore*, and then jerk off. Just don't jerk off to *The Jersey Shore*. That's unforgivable.

➤ OPTION #2

Get over it. Look, all the protesters smell. Everything is relative. Remember when you were in college? You would go a whole semester without showering. Start reliving your youth by being a pig filled with optimism and hope.

> **OPTION #3**

Hose them down. Start a mobile wash system. Surely you can't be the only one there who cares about personal hygiene. Get some bottles of body wash and a hose and start a human car wash. You'll still be standing up for what you believe in while saving the rest of the city from the stench. You're a hero!

> **OPTION #4**

Flip the switch. If someone wants to know why you're well rested and clean, tell them to mind their damn business. You can be dedicated to something without defecating on the street. Then accuse them of being the 1

percent of the 99 percent of the occupy protestors.

YOU MIGHT NEED A SHOWER IF . . .

- When you take a shit, the bathroom smells the same as it did before
- You use the oil from your hair instead of olive oil to cook dinner
- You are in college

3. A medical marijuana shop is about to open on your block.

Sure you smoked a little in college. But that was then. Now you are a responsible person who can no longer spend the weekend getting stoned and watching reruns of *Beavis and Butthead*. You have a job, a house, and a family. Then one night on your way home from work, you notice that a marijuana dispensary has opened for business, right down the street from your house. There goes the neighborhood.

The WTF Approach to Dealing with F*#!-ing Stoners on Your Block

➤ OPTION #1

Smoke up, bro. What are you waiting for? If it's legal in your state, then get on the pot train and go. Get to the doctor and get your medical marijuana card. When he asks why you need it, tell him you are experiencing anxiety over the medical marijuana dispensary on your street and need something to deal with the stress.

➤ OPTION #2

If you can't beat them, join them. Whether you like it or not, medical marijuana is growing in popularity and there's a lot of money to be made. If people will pay for legalized marijuana, why shouldn't you get some of that cash? Open a mini mart next to the dispensary, call it Bob Marley Munchies, and watch the stoners roll in. If you can't afford to open a store, just have "special" bake sales on your front lawn every day. Either way, you're sure to make a fortune.

> **OPTION #3**

Flip the switch. Start making and selling meth at your house. Shit, two can play at that game. Sure, it's not legal, but you'll probably make a lot more money than you would with a legit start-up. Start creating your own meth recipes, like meth mashed potatoes and meth mints. Meth addicts deserve fresh breath, too.

JUST ADD WEED

You can put pot into anything. Here are some things that only get better when you add pot:

- Cannbutter
- Pot hot chocolate
- Weed pizza
- College girls

HOW TO GET YOUR MEDICAL MARIJUANA CARD

- Chemo
- Cataracts
- Chronic back pain
- In-laws

WTFACT: Denver now appears to have more marijuana dispensaries than liquor stores, Starbucks coffee shops, or public schools, according to city and corporate records.—*The Denver Post*

What's the big deal, anyway? Why shouldn't pot be legal? Alcohol is legal and just look how many crimes are related to that. The only thing you expect from a stoner is the possibility of them eating all your food. Truth is, if more people smoked pot there would be fewer violent crimes— stoners are way too unmotivated to put the effort into committing a crime.

4. You're a gay man who wants to get married, but it's illegal in your state.

You and Bob are happy. You own a home together, you own a business together, you have sex with each other. You are partners in every way except one: You can't get married. WTF to do when you feel it's your right be just as miserable as your heterosexual peers?

The WTF Approach to Making Your Gay Love Legal

➤ OPTION #1

Wait. It's only a matter of time until your lame state passes the law allowing you to tie the knot. Look, you've waited this long, so what's another few years. In the meantime, keep banging other dudes on the side. You haven't made any vows to God yet; take advantage of this while you can.

➤ OPTION #2

Fight it. If your state's not moving fast enough for you, get on that gay high horse and go to city hall and fight this shit. Start a protest and a march. Hell, start a parade if you have to. Bring signs and flags; everyone knows the gays love their parades!

> **OPTION #3**

Get a sex change. If the law says "man and woman," then do something about it. Turn that penis into a vagina and get hitched. Careful, though. Once you become a woman your partner might not want you anymore. Not to worry; if your rack is big enough you'll have your choice of men to choose from.

> **OPTION #4**

Do it anyway. Send the invitations, get the rings, register at Bed Bath & Beyond, and have a big fabulous party. Who cares if you don't have a marriage certificate? Everyone knows weddings are all about the gifts. Then when the marriage doesn't work out, you can split and avoid filing any annoying divorce paperwork. Win-win!

WTF RANT

People who are gay should be outraged. While it is still not legal in some states to marry a same-sex partner, some lunatics are getting the okay to marry an object in our country and across the world. Check out these freaks and their beloved inanimate partners:

- In 2008, Erika La Tour Eiffel said "I do" to the Eiffel Tower in France surrounded by friends and family. Then Erika went ahead and took the iron structure's last name.
- Amy Wolfe of the UK has had a sexual relationship with and plans to marry a magic carpet fairground ride.
- A woman in Wyoming lobbied to marry a building to save it from demolition. The marriage was eventually overturned because it turned out the building is gay.
- According to Wikipedia, village elders forced an Indonesian teenager from Bali to marry a cow after he was caught having sex with it. Ngurah Alit claimed the cow seduced him and "wooed him with flattering compliments." The cow was then drowned in a "cleansing" ritual.

5. The CEO pays less in taxes than you.

Everyone hates paying taxes. Nothing feels worse than handing over your hard-earned money to Uncle Sam. In a perfect world there would be no taxes, everyone free to keep all of their pay. But when you find out that your multimillionaire CEO is taxed at half the rate you are, giving away 15 percent of his money compared to your 30 percent, you just about lose it. You make $50,000 a year and he makes $10,000,000? WTF?

The WTF Approach to Dealing with Getting F*#!-ed by Uncle Sam

> **OPTION #1**

Apologize to God for being a communist. Get on your knees right now and beg God's forgiveness for advocating class warfare. Right now Ronald Regan is shaking his head in heaven. How dare you!

> **OPTION #2**

Become a job creator. See, not so easy to build a company, is it, tough guy? That's why it's only fair that the rich guys pay less. Job creators are a special class of people put here on Earth to help lowly workers like you by building companies and creating jobs. They shouldn't be punished by high taxes. They shouldn't pay taxes at all. In fact, all the workers who benefit from their generosity should get in line to kiss the asses of each and every one of those rich pricks. That means you, buddy.

➤ OPTION #3

Vote for Obama. He's not perfect (he did choose to keep the Bush tax cuts in place the first go around), but at least he does not believe that rich people should pay a lower rate than regular schmucks like you.

➤ OPTION #4

Vote for Ron Paul. There will be no taxes at all, for rich or for poor. True, there will be no roads or schools or police or fireman and we will live in some post-apocalyptic world of total anarchy, but at least you get to keep all of your pay—if you survive.

➤ OPTION #5

Move to any European country other than Greece. Yes, Europe has even higher taxes than we do. But, unlike us, they like to spend their tax money on providing free health and dental insurance for all, improvements in transportation and infrastructure, and even help with day care. Doesn't that sound like a slightly better policy than starting unnecessary wars, bailing out banks, and building jet fighters for a cold war that ended twenty years ago?

WTFACT: The top marginal tax rate in 1952 was 90 percent under Republican President Dwight D. Eisenhower. In 2009 it was 35 percent under President Obama. Commie bastard!

6. You go to a Tea Party meeting expecting tea.

Your friends have been talking about the Tea Party meeting they've been going to. Apparently the meeting is somewhat political in nature, but as a middle-of-the-road kind of guy you don't really worry about that. But you do love tea, so why the hell not? And if you don't agree with everything that is discussed, as least you'll have some refreshment, but when you get there, there's only water. No finger sandwiches, no mini cakes, and no tea. How the F do you survive a Tea Party get together when there's no tea?

The WTF Approach to Not Getting What You Came to Get

➤ OPTION #1

Make some. You're probably either meeting at someone's home or a restaurant, so ask them to brew up a pot of tea. If they say they have none, offer to go get some. This is a tea party, damn it. You're entitled to tea.

➤ OPTION #2

Change the name of the group. If all they have is water, call this meeting the H2O group. Or the fringe lunatic group convinced the president is a Nazi.

➤ OPTION #3

Start a debate about why there's no damn tea at this Tea Party gathering. When someone tries to change the subject, bring it back to the tea. You came here for tea and you're not leaving until you get some.

➤ OPTION #4

Switch to coffee. Some believe conservatives are so closed minded they are scared of trying anything new. Well, prove those people wrong, switch to coffee and show then that even though you came expecting tea you are willing to be flexible.

IN THE FUTURE . . .

Have the gatherings at your place; that way you'll have tea!

THE TEA PARTY IS NO LAUGHING MATTER

- "At a Tea Party rally in Boston yesterday, Sarah Palin praised the crowd for winning that Senate race in Massachusetts. She said: 'Shoot, look at what you did in January. You shook up the United States Senate.' Unfortunately, no one heard the Senate thing, because after she said 'shoot,' 300 guns went off."— Jimmy Fallon
- "Well, tomorrow in Nashville, Sarah Palin will speak at the Tea Party Convention. Tickets are $550 apiece. Where are they getting this tea, Starbucks?"— Jay Leno

7. You want to run for office, but you've never had an affair.

Usually when someone runs for office they hire someone to make sure all those nasty skeletons don't fall out of the closet. But in your case the only thing anyone will find is that you have some unpaid parking tickets. That's it. No girlfriend on the side, no hooker you frequent, not even a love child. And you call yourself a politician? Where's the drama? The intrigue? The public apology with crocodile tears and a wife seething with hatred standing by her man? What to do when you really are squeaky clean.

The WTF Approach to Being Faithful to Your Wife While Running for Office

➤ OPTION #1

Start screwing. It's almost like a rite of passage to have a little something on the side, so get to it. People might distrust you more if they can't find any good dirt on you. Keep it quiet of course until you're elected.

➤ OPTION #2

Write a book. Write a book about how to be a politician and faithful to your wife. People will think it's fiction, of course, but shit, if you sell enough, you won't even have to run for office; you can retire and then find a hottie to have an affair with who only wants you 'cause you're a famous author.

➤ OPTION #3

Get your ass to the gym. Everybody knows chicks love a man in power—unless he's a big fatty. If you have any kind of power and no one has thrown themselves at you, you must really be carrying around some extra junk in your trunk. So cut down on the value meals, take the stairs every once in a while, and maybe you'll have better luck scoring with some power-hungry political groupie types.

for the ladies . . .

Do nothing. Even if you have an affair, no one will ever know; in extramarital affairs we screw; never talk.

WTF MATCHING GAME: MATCH THE POLITICIAN TO THE SCANDAL

1. Bill Clinton
2. Anthony Weiner
3. John Edwards
4. Jim McGreevy
5. John F. Kennedy
6. Eliot Spitzer
7. Arnold Schwarzenegger

A. Likes the dumb blondes
B. Supports the oldest profession in the world
C. "Came" out of the closet
D. Stained a blue dress
E. Reproduces with the help
F. Likes sending dick pics
G. Cheated on someone dying of cancer

Answers: 1. D; 2. F; 3. G; 4. C; 5. A; 6. B; 7. E

POLITICAL SCANDALS ARE NO LAUGHING MATTER

- Q: How many Republican politicians can you fit in the closet?
- A: Evidently, all of them.

It's no wonder these politicians have affairs. If they weren't in power no one would want to screw them. Everyone knows politics is show business for ugly people.

QUOTES FROM NOTORIOUS POLITICAL DOGS

- "If I don't have a woman every three days or so I get a terrible headache."
  —President John Kennedy
- "Too many good docs are getting out of the business. Too many OB-GYNs aren't able to practice their love with women all across this country."
  —President George W. Bush

8. Your manufacturing job gets shipped overseas.

It's a story you've heard a lot over the last few years but figured it would never happen to you. You and your workers are so dedicated, so committed to making a quality product. And the company is making money hand over fist. Hell, you and your team haven't received an increase in pay in years. How much money do these corporate schmucks, need?

The WTF Approach to Seeing Your F*#!-ing Job Go to China

➤ OPTION #1

Go back to school. The manufacturing job market will continue to decline, as it's cheaper to send these jobs to China and other places overseas. Go back to school and become a lawyer. There's always jobs for those assholes.

➤ OPTION #2

Work for slave wages. To get your job back, you are going to have to work for less than a worker will take in China. You know you could lose a few pounds, anyhow.

➤ OPTION #3

Vote within your economic interest. Stop voting for candidates based on whether or not they go to church and don't cheat on their wife and start voting for candidates that will fight for policies that are in your economic interest. Vote for someone who instead of giving tax breaks for companies that take their business overseas will offer tax incentives for companies to make their products right here at home in the USA. What a crazy idea, eh?

IN THE FUTURE . . .

Be born in China. Not in the near future, but in the next twenty years or so. Be sure to be born a boy though, so your mother isn't forced to leave you to die as an infant in the middle of the Gobi Desert. Animals.

9. Your unemployment benefits are running out.

You've tried everything. You've asked around. You've sent out resumes. You've applied in person. But times really are tough. In this Great Recession getting a job and keeping it is harder than it's been in a long, long time. With your unemployment benefits about to run out you are starting to really get worried. You've already sold your car, your child, and your own ass on the street. What now?

The WTF Approach to Being F*#!-ing Jobless

> **OPTION #1**

Become a pimp. Why sell your own ass when you can sell the asses of others? It's a much cooler job than the one you had as a graphic designer many moons ago. And, even if you can't seem to make it work, at least you can say "It's hard out here for a pimp" when times are hard. Sounds much cooler than "It's hard out here for a graphic designer."

> **OPTION #2**

Sell apples, just like out-of-work people did in the Great Depression. Of course, you'll have to compete with the illegal aliens to break into this business.

➤ OPTION #3

Start a blog. Start a website like *Texts from Last Night*, only about your life as a depressed and hopelessly unemployed slob. Become famous for creating a venue for people to vent in this trying time. If your life is falling apart, why not make the most of it? Some potential titles you can name your site:

- Things My Social Worker Says
- Stuff Laid-Off People Like
- The Job/Job Project

➤ OPTION #4

One word: McDonald's. If you're lucky . . .

➤ OPTION #5

Get a time machine and go back to a time when the economy was booming and the only thing the nation worried about was the president's penis.

for the ladies . . .

Marry someone—quick. Sure, you probably wanted to marry for love, but times are tough. Find a man with a good job stat!

WTF: UP CLOSE AND PERSONAL

I was once fired for leaving out the turkey on a turkey sandwich from Einstein's Bagels. I was a sweet kid. Not particularly sharp, mind you, but sweet.

—GB

10. You go overseas and everyone hates you for being an American.

For an American, going overseas is tricky business. Sometimes you go somewhere where they love you, sometimes you go somewhere where they hate you, but nowhere you go will they be indifferent. No matter where you go on this Earth, the American traveler is forced into some sort of political discussion about the reach and use of American power. So much for vacation. WTF?

The WTF Approach to Being a F*#!-ing American Overseas

➤ OPTION #1

Tell them to shut the fuck up. Do your best Clint Eastwood expression and tell them that you'll kill them if they utter another word. Nobody fucks with America, asshole!

➤ OPTION #2

Say you're from Canada. This was a popular thing for American tourists to do in the Bush era, when the world really hated our guts. Once you say you're Canadian, you will finally get that indifference you always craved.

You'll be judged by the content of your character, not your nationality. Because, really, who gives a fuck about Canada?

➤ OPTION #3

Lecture them. Give them a lecture about the importance of American hegemony to foster a peaceful, stable global economy. Tell them about all the good things American power has accomplished, like saving their ass in WWI and WWII. If they want a more recent example tell them about the War in Kosovo, a genocide that would have continued right in the backyard of the Western European powers. Make sure to leave out the less positive stuff like the Spanish-American War, The Mexican-American War, Vietnam, Iraq, Afghanistan, Grenada, arming the Contra guerillas with weapons sales to Iran, etc.

➤ OPTION #4

Flip the switch. Don't they realize our country is pretty shitty right now? Start giving them attitude for not being American. "Oh poor you, you're Chinese, aren't you from the most powerful country in the world?" "I feel so bad for you French people, with your universal health care and all." Them tell them to shut the fuck up!

for the ladies . . .
Play nice, they stone women in other countries.

TOP REASONS OTHER COUNTRIES HATE AMERICA

1. We think we're the center of the universe.
2. We win everything.
3. We eat everything.
4. We make and have nukes.
5. We meddle in everyone else's affairs.
6. We created Jerry Springer and Paris Hilton.

11. You're the only liberal working at Fox News.

Y̲ou've been out of work for months and you need a job. You've been trying to hold out, but now things are getting desperate, so when you get offered the perfect job as an editor at a cable news station you jump for joy. The pay is amazing and benefits are fantastic. Then you hear the catch: the network is Fox News. Oh no. You're a die-hard liberal and everyone knows that Fox is not exactly "fair and balanced" as they claim. You want to stay true to your political beliefs, but you also want to eat.

The WTF Approach to Working on the Right When You're a Leftie

> **OPTION #1**

Embrace it. It's a fact that all the news anchors that work at Fox News are, well, foxes. In fact you can't remember ever flipping through the channel and seeing an unattractive female correspondent on FOX News. So what if they're

conservative. Go there and land yourself some right-wing ass.

> **OPTION #2**

Play both sides. So you're not a conservative; who gives a shit? You're working as an editor. Nobody cares which way you swing. When someone tries to talk about politics at work just tell them you're so busy and can't get into it right now. Then go out after work with your liberal friends and rip all those right wingers apart. At least you'll be able to pay for your drinks now.

➤ OPTION #3

Switch sides. It's happens all the time, just look at Dennis Miller. This comic was a die-hard liberal, then one day, bam! Conservative. No one seems to really give a shit, and he still makes millions of dollars.

WHY IS THE RIGHT SO HOT? SO HOT CONSERVATIVE WOMEN

- Megan Kelly—Fox News
- Michele Bachmann, former candidate for Republican nomination for president
- Jill Dobson, former Fox News correspondent; host, *The Jill Dobson Show*
- Martha Washington—the first First Lady

NOT-SO-HOT LIBERAL WOMEN

- Nancy Pelosi—minority leader of the House of Representatives; former Speaker of the House
- Hillary Clinton—secretary of state
- Rosie O'Donnell—talk show host

12. You are the 1 percent.

It's not your fault you were born into money. Turns out your family has been in the laxative business for generations, generating a small fortune that is soon to be yours. You never thought of this as a bad thing until you started hearing all this noise about the 1 percent blah blah blah. Why are the other 99 percent hating on you?

The WTF Approach to Enjoying Your F*#!-ing 1 Percent Life

> **OPTION #1**

Give it away. Donate your fortune to a good cause like ending leprosy or giving every woman free breast implants.

> **OPTION #2**

Enjoy it. Start hanging out with other 1 percenters and have some fun. Screw those other people. The truth is they're just jealous that

they don't have that money. If they did, they would be right there with you on the beach in the south of France sipping a mai tai and telling jokes about poor people.

> **OPTION #3**

Go riding. No, not horseback riding. Just riding. Only poor people say "horseback riding." Rich people like you who have several horses say "riding." It's just yet another way to sound like an asshole.

➤ OPTION #4

Get a yacht. Strap on your yachting shoes and sail around the world, spreading the gospel of lower taxes for the wealthy and lax environmental standards for companies polluting the air and water.

YOU MIGHT BE A 1 PERCENTER IF . . .
- When you are sick, you call a doctor

YOU MIGHT BE A 99 PERCENTER IF . . .
- When you are sick, you call a priest

YOU MIGHT BE A 1 PERCENTER IF . . .
- You are just so over Paris

YOU MIGHT BE A 99 PERCENTER IF . . .
- You are just so over Paris, Texas

YOU MIGHT BE A 1 PERCENTER IF . . .
- You refer to horseback riding simply as "riding"

YOU MIGHT BE A 99 PERCENTER IF . . .
- You used to have a horse—until you had to eat it

chapter two

over the borderline

13. You live in Arizona and you're scared of guns.

>>>>> You love Arizona. The sweltering sun, the blinding sand-storms, the almost limitless amount of cheap illegal labor. What's not to love? And let's not forget about the cacti. You gotta love the cacti. What a great word, cacti. One of the best plural nouns of all time. The plural and singular moose is another good one. What to do when you're a pussy who talks about plural nouns while everyone else in Arizona is strapped and ready to bust a cap in your nerdy ass?

The WTF Approach to Facing Your Fear of F*#!-ing Guns

➤ OPTION #1

Make love, not war. During sex, you release serotonin, the pleasure chemical that puts you in that euphoric state of mind. The more you have sex, the better you will feel; soon you won't give a shit about your neighbor and his six-pack of shotguns unless you start

screwing his wife, then kiss your ass goodbye.

➤ OPTION #2

Move to civilization. Try Denmark or Switzerland or Sweden. Or all the "socialist" places that Americans think suck but are actually really, really nice. True you won't find Arby's in any of those places, but you also won't get shot in the face either. And even if you do, you can actually go to the doctor without foreclosing on your home the next day.

> **OPTION #3**

Bite the bullet. Learn to love guns. Go to a firing range and practice shooting. Apparently firing a gun is quite a power trip. You might even meet a cute girl there, and chicks with guns are hot! So buy yourself a pretty little hand gun and carry it with you at all times.

> **OPTION #4**

If moving isn't an option and you just can't get on board with the fire arms law, then do something about it from the inside. Run for office and get elected so you can change the law. Or at least sleep with an intern and show her how big your "weapon" is.

OTHER COUNTRIES THAT ARE ALSO ANTI-GUNS

- England
- Ireland
- New Zealand

THE RIGHT TO BE AN ASSHOLE

Look, this nation—particularly the West—loves guns. Guns are a part of our history. And we have a right to own one, according to the Second Amendment. But what kind of guns can we own? The Second Amendment reads "the right of the people to keep and bear Arms shall not be infringed." Well, what constitutes "Arms"? Tanks and Fighter Jets and Nuclear Missiles are "arms"—is that what the Founding Fathers meant? Probably not. No, they meant that everyone could have a musket that took about a half hour to load. Too bad we have semiautomatic assault rifles instead of muskets today. If we did, the Columbine lunatics would have been bum rushed before they could have gotten off a shot. Careful of the bayonet.

*WTF*ACT: In Arizona you do not have to have a permit to carry a concealed hand-gun. Seriously, WTF?

14. You get pulled over by the cops in Arizona and your last name is Lopez.

Ay dios mio! Was that a cop? Where was he hiding? You hear the sirens and pull over. He looks at your license, looks at you, and looks at the license again. You are in Arizona and your last name is Lopez. You're fucked.

The WTF Approach to Being Mexican in F*#!-ing Arizona

➤ OPTION #1

Think fast. Tell the cops you took your wife's name. Your "maiden" name is Smith, a good old American name. But it's the twenty-first century and you wanted to support your wife. Now you'll just have to prove that she's not illegal. Damn.

➤ OPTION #2

Play the celebrity card. Yes Lopez is your last name, as in George Lopez—your brother. Offer the cop that you usually don't tell a lot of people that because they always wants free tickets to shows. Yes, even his.

➤ OPTION #3

Flip the switch. Ask this cop what his last name is. O'Donnell, eh? What a drunk! Sure, you'll end up in jail, but at least you made your point.

➤ OPTION #4

Do nothing. Remember, you are not an illegal, even if people treat you like you are.

WTFACT: Stupid laws in America: In Oklahoma, it is illegal to have a sleeping donkey in your bathtub after 7 P.M.

15. You run out of peyote during a vision quest in Sedona.

Sedona, Arizona, has been a hotspot for new-age bohemian types for decades. Thousands of so-called "spiritual" people head out to Sedona in search of enlightenment. Some are on a vision quest to find their spirit animal. Some just want to get in a good hike and take in the view. And then there are others who take their spiritual life more seriously. The ones that seek the same experience the Native Americans did when they came here to feed their soul. But that takes peyote. And after finally scoring some you sit down on one of the red rock buttes, look in your knapsack for the peyote, and . . . it's gone! You can't believe it! The last time you checked it was right between your Bhagavad Gita and your pack of granola bars. WTF?

The WTF Approach to Having No F*#!-ing Peyote

➤ STEP #1

Stay Calm. The whole point of this trip was to get in touch with nature and not to freak out about everything like you do at home. Relax, breathe in the hot, dry, disgusting desert air, and exhale all the stress and sadness that has brought you on this ridiculous journey.

> **STEP #2**

Find another peyote partier. There's plenty of other weirdos like you out there. Who knows, you might even meet a hot bohemian chick with a handful of peyote powder and a mouthful of armpit hair. Party on!

> **STEP #3**

Do without it. Cross your legs, close your eyes, and breathe in deeply. Feel the wind in your hair, the sun on your face. Now, meditate for a few hours until you space out completely. Now you can falsely attribute a nonthinking mental state as some grand cosmic conception of "enlightenment."

> **STEP #4**

Masturbate. No particular reason except that the image of someone jerking off on a cliff in Sedona is really funny.

> **WTFACT:** Studies have shown that peyote doesn't damage your brain over time. According to Dr. John Halpern, associate director of substance abuse research at McLean Hospital in Belmont, Massachusetts, they weren't able to find any real mental deficits. He then went on to say only the alcoholics showed signs of brain problems. Maybe because they're alcoholics, duh?

Other creative uses of the word *peyote*:

Peyote Ugly: A human being so repugnant that no amount of mind-altering substances could possibly make him or her attractive.

Peyote Orgasm: When an orgasm is so good you immediately fall into a state of semiconscious hallucinogenic bliss.

Peyote Penis: When you take so many drugs you think your dick is bigger than it really is.

16. You live in Roswell, New Mexico, and don't believe in aliens.

You've heard the story your whole life: On July 2, 1947, in Roswell, New Mexico, an object crash-landed on a ranch approximately seventy-five miles northwest of Roswell. The local air base at Roswell investigated, and a week later the Roswell Army Air Field (RAAF) announced it had recovered a "flying disk." A couple of hours after the announcement the U.S. Army Air Force officials stated that it was not a UFO but a weather balloon. Sounds reasonable, right? Well, not to your friends and family in Roswell, all of whom believe that aliens are still being held alive deep in a cave in the New Mexican desert. But you've never bought all this extraterrestrial nonsense. You hated *ET*, despised *Independence Day*, and thought *The X-Files* was total bullshit. What to do when you're surrounded by people who want to be probed?

The WTF Approach to Life on Other F*#!-ing Planets

➤ OPTION #1

Change the debate. Focus on illegal aliens. The big issue right now in New Mexico and the border states is illegal aliens, not extraterrestrial aliens.

➤ OPTION #2

Read *Communion*. This supposedly true account of a writer abducted by aliens is one of the scariest fucking stories ever. Stop being so closed minded and accept the fact that we are probably not the only intelligent beings in an infinite universe. Read this book and you'll believe in aliens by the end of it.

➤ OPTION #3

Investigate it. Prove to these lunatics that aliens don't exist and the only kind of anal probing going on out in the desert is between two consenting adults. Do the research so you have facts to back this up. Become the Stephen Hawking of the extraterrestrial research.

➤ OPTION #4

Screw with them. Start telling people that you are an alien that came down to Earth to study humans. In fact, tell them there are thousands of you here on Earth posing as humans to gain knowledge and soon the rest of your kind will be coming to take over. Watch them ask for an autograph—and then shit their pants.

SYMPTOMS OF BEING ABDUCTED BY ALIENS (OR JUST A GREAT NIGHT OF PARTYING? YOU DECIDE.)

- Missing time
- Nightmares
- Unexplained bruising
- Sore ass

WTF: UP CLOSE AND PERSONAL

My grandmother's copy of *Communion* used to scare the shit out of me. The alien on the cover had these big, black cat-shaped eyes—the eyes of pure evil. The book, which stood erect half-opened on the living room table, used to beckon me in the middle of the night. It taunted me, daring me to face him and stare into his coal-black eyes. If I didn't, he said he would come into my room and kill me. So, my hands trembling with fear, I left my bedroom and braved the long, dark hallway to the living room. Getting closer, I closed my eyes, took a deep breath and clenched my fists. This was it, the big alien showdown. Boy versus beast. Inches away from the book, I opened my eyes, half-expecting the intergalactic monster to jump out of the book and devour my eight-year old face. He didn't. I exhaled and smiled triumphantly. The night belonged to me. I then went into my room, tried—unsuccessfully—to ejaculate to an image of Paula Abdul, and went to sleep; only to do it all over again the next day.

—GB

17. You get caught swimming across the Rio Grande to Mexico in search of a job.

They are calling it the Great Recession, but you just call it the reason you are out of work, upside down on your mortgage, and forced to consider giving your body to science. Not when you're dead, but now. What's an out-of-work American to do? One day you learn that despite all this paranoia over illegal immigrants crossing the border to the United States, statistics show they're not coming anymore or not nearly at the rate before the Great Recession. Hmm, maybe things are getting better in Mexico? You decide to give Mexican life a shot. You grab a poncho, a bottle of tequila, some flippers, and a Spanish/English dictionary and head across the Rio Grande. But just as your hands reach the promised land, the golden Mexican soil, you look up to find a Mexican border patrol guard (Si, they have them as well). Adios amigos. What now?

The WTF Approach to Getting F*#!-ing into Mexico

➤ OPTION #1

Hasta La Vista, Baby! Make a run for it and dive back into the river. Swim desperately and get back to American soil pronto. Even Texas is better than a Mexican jail. Barely.

➤ OPTION #2

Bribe him. The good thing about an intrinsically corrupt country is that you can bribe your way out of almost anything. Offer him twenty and a blow job and he'll not only let you stay in Mexico, but he'll be your amigo for life.

➤ OPTION #3

Answer his questions. Maybe he just wants to ask you a few things.

Namely, *what the fuck are you doing swimming to Mexico, gringo? Stupido!*

➤ OPTION #4

Play dumb. Pretend that you have no have idea how you got you there. Maybe fake a mental illness. Explain how you forgot to take your meds and this sometimes happens.

IT'S ALL GRINGO TO ME

There are several theories on the origin of the Spanish word "gringo." One is that it began during the Mexican-American war when American troops, who wore green, were taunted with Mexican cries of "Green go!" Another theory says the term comes from a popular song sung by American frontiersmen "Green Grow the Lilacs." However, the most accepted etymological theory of gringo comes from the Spanish word griego, which means "Greek." Just like we say in English "It's all Greek to me" to explain something inexplicable, the Spanish also have a saying, habla en griego, or "to speak Greek" to refer to something foreign and incomprehensible.

chapter three

the fly-over
states

18. Your car breaks down on Route 50 and you have no cell reception.

You're finally doing it, that coast-to-coast cross-country trip you've been planning for years. Starting at the Atlantic Ocean, ending at the Pacific Ocean. This is gonna be great. Just you, the radio, and open road. You're halfway there, driving that famous Highway 50, when somewhere on the 110-mile stretch between Texas and Nevada you hear a sound. You turn up the radio and try to ignore it, but then you hear it again, then you feel your car slowing down. It stops in the middle of nowhere. You try your cell, but to no avail. No bars, no signal, nothing. Suddenly your dream trip has turned into a nightmare. WTF can you do when your car breaks down in the middle of nowhere and you are all alone?

The WTF Approach to Surviving in the Middle of F*#!-ing Nowhere

> **OPTION #1**

Start walking. That's right, start moving until you reach a part when you can get a signal. Or until you fall down from exhaustion. Bring some water or a weapon just in case; you never know what you might run into. If a guy can make it for 127 hours stuck in a rock you can walk 75 miles no problem, so start moving buddy.

> **OPTION #2**

Start a fire. Look for something to burn, other than your car, and light it up. Hopefully someone will see the smoke and come out to investigate. And, hey, if you happen to know smoke signals try that too. Shoot, I'm sure there must be some Indians somewhere around there.

> **OPTION #3**

Set up camp. Maybe the universe is trying to tell you something. Maybe this is where you are supposed to be. Claim your land and make yourself a home there. Sure, you might starve to death or die from boredom, but at least you won't have any of those annoying neighbors to bother you.

➤ OPTION #4

Make out your will. Face it; you're screwed. It could be days until another car passes by, and by then your cell phone will be dead. And if you don't die from starvation the wild animals are sure to get you.

IN THE FUTURE . . .

Take a plane or at least a friend; that way if you break down you won't die alone. And if your friend dies first, you can always eat him to stay alive. Food for thought.

WTF: UP CLOSE AND PERSONAL

My car once broke down in the middle of nowhere. It would not start. I was hungry; I was cold; I was terrified. My life flashed before my eyes. I have never felt more alone, more without hope. It was the worst fifteen minutes of my life. Thanks AAA.

—JM

19. You can't find a decent potato during a stay in Boise.

When you think of Idaho you think of one thing: No, not white supremacist groups hiding out in the mountains and training for the inevitable race war (although they are out there)—you inevitably think about the potato. But to your surprise, you can't seem to find a decent potato in all of Boise. What's up?

The WTF Approach to Finding a Great Spud

> **OPTION #1**

Blame the Chinese. China is now the world's largest potato producer. (Think about *that* the next time you order "freedom" fries.) And given China's reputation for corporate espionage and trickster moves, might it be foul play? Look into it. You can never trust those sneaky bastards.

> **OPTION #2**

Two words: Bacon bits. Who cares how bad the potato is? Everything taste better with bacon. Bake the shitty potato, melt some cheddar cheese on top, and then bust out the sour cream, chives, and bacon bits. If it still tastes bad, see a doctor immediately.

WTFACT: A New World crop, the potato was introduced to Europe by the Spanish after they conquered the Incas. At first crushed by the defeat and the slaughter of many of their citizens, the Peruvian people forgave the Europeans after having their first taste of potatoes au gratin. True story.

WTFACT: The Irish Potato Famine was not as bad as people make it out to be. Sure 750,000 Irish were confirmed dead between 1845 and 1851 as a result of this potato blight, but that's God's way of thinning out the herd, so to speak. Truth is, this is probably where people learned that carbohydrates kill, and possibly because of this famine we now have the Akins diet. Thank you, Ireland!

IN THE FUTURE . . .

Don't go to Boise, Idaho. Seriously, why would you?

WTFACT: French Fries were introduced to the United States when Thomas Jefferson served them in the White House during his presidency of 1801–1809. Serving French fries and having children with his slave? Wow. He *was* a great president!

for the ladies . . .

What are you doing eating potatoes anyway?! Lay off the carbs, bitch!

Some foods aren't what they seem when it comes to the four food groups. For instance many people think potatoes are in the grains group.

Potato: Vegetable group
Tomato: Fruit group
Oats: Grains group
Sperm: Protein group

20. You go to Brokeback Mountain looking to get lucky but find only squirrels.

Brokeback Mountain changed your life. You couldn't get those images out of your mind. The vast untouched beauty of the West was awe-inspiring: snow-capped mountains, trees as tall as skyscrapers, roaring rivers, quiet streams. It was beautiful. Add to that two guys banging the shit out of one another and you were sold. "I'm heading west," you whispered aloud in the theater, one hand in your popcorn bucket, the other on your cock. So you packed up your shit the next day and headed out across the country, finally reaching the legendary party hotspot, Brokeback Mountain. But when you got there you didn't see anyone. Where the hell are all the hot horny cowboys? Turns out that after two days of camping at Brokeback the only thing you saw was a squirrel. WTF?

The WTF Approach to Getting F*#!-ing Laid on a Famous Mountain

➤ OPTION #1

Reflect on your life. This might be a good thing. You can use this time to re-evaluate your choices, like the choice to drive hours to the middle of nowhere looking for cowboy butt. Try to enjoy the peace and quiet of nature while you masturbate furiously to the image of a naked Heath Ledger riding a bear.

➤ OPTION #2

Call one of your friends to come up for some outdoor sex. If none of your friends lives nearby call for some takeout. Hopefully you get some young, cute pizza guy to come out there to your cabin.

➤ OPTION #3

Keep heading west. Eventually you'll get to a place where you can have all the gay sex you ever dreamed of. It's a place called San Francisco.

IN THE FUTURE . . .

Use an app like Grinder to help you find where the men are. Grinder is an app for your phone that lets you see where all the gay dudes are up to a five-mile radius.

There's no beating around the bush when it comes to gay bars (literally NO BUSH). The names of these bars are so obvious that you know exactly what you're getting. Just consider:

- 3-Legged Cowboy, Atlanta
- Mother Load, San Francisco
- The Closet, Chicago
- Dicks, New York

21. You Live in Green Bay and you hate football.

Some cities are synonymous with one thing. D.C. with politics. Hollywood with the movie business. West Palm Beach for people who are dying. In Green Bay, Wisconsin, it's all about football. This city of only 100,000 people is the proud home of the Green Bay Packers, one of American football's oldest and most successful teams. Green Bay residents live, breathe, and sometimes even have sex with football. But you aren't into the sport. And as a consequence, no one is into you.

The WTF Approach to Dealing with a Football-Crazed Town

➤ OPTION #1

Get drunk. You don't have to watch the game to watch the game. Get wasted and hit on chicks the whole time during football Sundays. You do like girls, don't you?

➤ OPTION #2

Study random facts. Just memorize a few obscure facts about the NFL so that by dropping these facts people think you like the game even if you aren't watching.

➤ OPTION #3

Date a cheerleader. At least you'll put that gay rumor to rest. Then when the game is on TV and everyone is talking about that "amazing pass" the quarterback just made, you can say, "sorry I didn't see that amazing pass, I was staring at my cheerleader girlfriend's "amazing ass."

➤ OPTION #4

Date a football player. Who cares if you're not gay, professional football players are really rich and they are good with their hands. Shit, you might just enjoy getting "tackled."

➤ OPTION #5: *What NOT to do:*

Become a Minnesota Vikings fan. You *will* be killed.

for the ladies . . .

Like whichever team the guy you like roots for, duh.

WTFACT: The Green Bay Packers are not owned by an individual as other teams are. Instead, it is owned by the fans. Green Bay Packers, Inc. has been a publicly owned, nonprofit corporation since August 18, 1923, the same year that Brett Favre retired for the first time.

AMERICA LOVES THEIR TEAMS: THE TOP FOUR FAN CLUBS

1. Boston Red Sox
2. Pittsburgh Steelers
3. Detroit Red Wings
4. Boston Celtics

Just proves the shittier the city the better the fans!

22. You live in Madison, Wisconsin, and are lactose intolerant.

Nobody, not even the French, love cheese like Wisconsiners. They go crazy for that shit. Everyone has seen Green Bay Packer fans sporting that ridiculous hat shaped like a giant piece of cheese. Everywhere you go in the state you can see people eating cheese curds out of a bag. But you never could participate in this native love of cheese. Born lactose intolerant, you have two choices: Avoid dairy products or shit your pants. After a couple years of thinking and shitting, you chose the latter. But what else to eat?

The WTF Approach to Being F*#!-ing Lactose Intolerant

➤ OPTION #1

Ask for federal protection. The state officials are not going to help you because they are just as cheese-obsessed as the general population. The only way to get protection from persecution by these cheese-eating fascists is to appeal directly to the federal government. Just like they stepped in to integrate the schools in the South, they'll help integrate you back into the cheese-eating society, whether these cheese heads like it or not.

➤ OPTION #2

Drown yourself in one of the state's 10,000 lakes. Or is that Minnesota? Well, who gives a shit? Wisconsin, Minnesota. Same shit.

➤ OPTION #3

Eliminate the source. Sneak into a cheese farm and contaminate all the cheese. Soon people will get sick (even die!) and the news media will send a shiver down each cheese-eatin' spine in the state. Cheese will be the enemy, not you.

for the ladies . . .

Use this to your advantage. The next time your guys ask for oral sex, tell him your lactose intolerant and you can't give a blowjob to anyone who consumes dairy.

WTFACT: The Chinese referred to Europeans as "smelly milk people" because of their love of cheese, which was unfamiliar to the Chinese diet. In response, Europeans took over their country and destroyed a proud nation. See, what goes around, comes around.

23. You live in Hell, Michigan, and it really, really sucks.

Know the saying "go to hell"? Well, you're already there. Hell, Michigan, to be exact. And it's just like hell—only cold as fuck. God this sucks. What the hell to do?

The WTF Approach to Living in F*#!-ing Hell

> **OPTION #1**

Become the Devil. Run for mayor as the Anti-Christ on a platform of retuning Hell to its former glory. Tell the people that you and your demonic angels will destroy God and all his white-winged halo whores.

> **OPTION #2**

Give up. Just give up and live in Hell for eternity just like every other local loser you know.

> **OPTION #3**

Move to the North Pole. Actually, North Pole, Minnesota, to be exact, which isn't very far away. It's also cold and boring, but at least you can chill with Santa instead of Satan.

> **OPTION #4**

Found your own town called "Heaven" and let all the good people of Hell move there, leaving the devilish trash behind. Why be a slave in Hell when you can be a ruler in Heaven?

24. You get locked out of your place in Chicago during the winter with no money and no coat.

Chicago is a great town. It's a town of jazz, deep-dish pizza, and, of course, the Chicago Cubs, the most lovable losers in baseball. There is so much to see. The Willis Tower, the Drake Hotel, and the birthplace of dynamic duo, Leopold and Loeb. But there is one downside to living in Chicago, as any Chicagoan will admit: it's the coldest fucking place on Earth.

Not bad—if you're bundled up. But after running out to get the mail in a sweat suit you get back to your door to notice one thing. It's fucking locked. Holy shit . . .

The WTF Approach to Surviving a Chicago Winter

> **OPTION #1**

Scream for help and maybe someone will take pity on you. On the other hand, Chicago has one of the highest crime rates in America, so don't be surprised

if people start running from you, rather than toward you.

> **OPTION #2**

Kill a furry animal. Even in the big city, there's got to be some wild animals roaming around that could make for a nice furry coat. Try the zoo. If you can't seem to capture a hairy animal, look around for some female members of the Occupy Chicago movement. You'll have enough hair to last three winters.

➤ OPTION #3

Treat others as you would wish to be treated. No direct relevance here, but it's a good rule of thumb in any situation.

➤ OPTION #4

Get smashed. Why do you think all those bums are drunk? Keeps them warm. On the other hand, it also keeps them from getting sober, getting off the street, and having a reason to live.

➤ OPTION #5

Shop lift. This is going to be tricky, but you can do it. Hide the coat in your pants. When they inevitably question you what you are hiding in your bulging pants just look embarrassed and say that mannequins turn you on. They'll understand.

IN THE FUTURE . . .

Wear a coat—always. Even in the humid, Midwestern summer.

for the ladies . . .

Ask someone to rub up against you to create body heat and prevent hypothermia. You'll be hot in no time.

25. You get kicked out of public office in Chicago for lack of corruption.

When you graduated Harvard Law school you had the world by the reins. Everyone expected you'd jump at the first high-paying job making gazillions of dollars. But you didn't. Public service, that's where it was at for you. So you passed up the cushy job in Washington and headed back to your hometown of Chicago. There you spent the next few years helping the poor and underprivileged communities of the Chicago area learn to organize themselves politically in order to help them be heard. Basically, you wasted your time. But eventually this paid off and you were elected to public office. Finally, you could make a difference! Finally, this notoriously corrupt city would have effective and honest leadership! Well, turns out you were wrong. Because the minute you start working for the people you get kicked out of office for lack of corruption. WTF?

The WTF Approach to Getting the Boot for Being F*#!-ing Honest

➤ OPTION #1

Take a closer look at state law. The good thing about a corrupt state like Illinois is that there must be a loophole in the law that gets around this "anti-anti-corruption" law you've supposedly violated.

➤ OPTION #2

Become corrupted. It happens to everyone eventually, you might as well do it now. Start by offering illegal bribes to get your newly corrupted ass back into office. Once you're in, be as corrupt as you can possibly be. Ask an expert like former governor, Rod Blagojevich. He'll help you out.

➤ OPTION #3

Go into show business. Get on *Celebrity Apprentice* and become a reality star. Way more money and power in that profession. With all that newfound fame, we're sure

you'll start fucking up. So when Hollywood kicks you out, you can run for office again. Americans love Hollywood stars who take office.

> "Chicago is unique. It is the only completely corrupt city in America."
>
> —Charles Edward Merriam

Chicago is not only known for corruption; here are some other fun facts:

- Has world's largest public library with a collection of more than 2 million books
- Has over thirty *Fortune* 500 companies
- Has oldest public zoo
- Can see four states from the Willis Tower (aka Sears Tower) Skydeck (Indiana, Illinois, Michigan, and Wisconsin)
- Birthplace of the Twinkie, 1930

26. Your car breaks down in Detroit.

On your way across country, you knew you had to stop in Detroit. It's a Great American city, home of the auto industry, Motown records, and some of the highest rates of rape and homicide in the nation. What's not to love? You were just going to do a little sightseeing during the day, and then head out to greener (and safer) pastures. But before you get to the hotel you get lost in a bad neighborhood and your car breaks down. Uh oh.

The WTF Approach to Being Stuck in the Middle of Detroit

➤ OPTION #1

Have someone rebuild it. Hey, you're in Motor City, aren't you? Of course, the American auto industry ain't what it used to be, but it's getting better after the bailout. If there is any place you should be able to get your car fixed in the United States, it should be in Detroit. Don't worry, there will be plenty of jobless ex-factory workers who will be eager to help.

➤ OPTION #2

Protect Ya Neck. In the immortal words of the Wu Tang Clan, "you best protect ya neck." Make sure to also protect the rest of your body too, especially your balls. Getting shot in the balls totally sucks.

➤ OPTION #3

Flip the switch. Start robbing fools left and right. Anyone you see. Soon everyone will be afraid of *you*. Start with old ladies who have trouble walking and then work your way up to teenage male gang members.

➤ OPTION #4

What NOT to do: Do not start walking around around the city asking people for help. That's like walking around wearing a sign that reads, "My car broke down and I have a wallet full of cash and no way to escape."

THE TOP ELEVEN MOST DANGEROUS CITIES IN AMERICA IN 2011 ACCORDING TO *FORBES*

1. You guessed it, Detroit is number 1
2. Memphis, Tennessee
3. Springfield, Illinois
4. Flint, Michigan
5. Anchorage, Alaska
6. Lubbock, Texas
7. Stockton, California
8. Tallahassee, Florida
9. Las Vegas, Nevada
10. Rockford, Illinois
11. Narnia. Any place where lions wander around freely must be badass!

27. You build a baseball diamond out of your Iowa cornfield but they never come.

"If you build it, they will come." Thus spoke the whisper from the sky. Remembering *Field of Dreams*, one of the few Kevin Costner movies you hadn't blocked from memory, you figure you are as lucky as that Iowan farmer. Turns out, property in Iowa isn't very expensive, and with all the money you'll be raking in from the ghost baseball games, it's a no brainer. So before long, you pack up your shit, head to Iowa, and buy a corn farm so you can turn it into a baseball diamond. Before you know it, you're sweeping the home base of your new baseball diamond . . . and then you wait. But unlike the movie, no one ever mysteriously appears from the corn fields. No one except the representative from the bank who's come to foreclose on your property. But you heard that damn voice. WTF?

The WTF Approach to F*#!-ing Up Your Cornfield

➤ OPTION #1

Start a team. You built a field, now build a team. Name your team after some random animal. Try to pick an intimidating animal like a Komodo dragon, not some pussy animal like a sea otter. Charge admission to the games and you'll make your money back in no time.

➤ OPTION #2

Offer up a sacrifice. If you are really willing to go all out and risk your family's financial future based on a voice from the sky, up the ante by offering a human being as a sacrifice to the gods. If you can, choose a banker.

➤ OPTION #3

Make up with your dead dad. The voice is a sign for you to forgive your dead father for not playing catch with you. Maybe he was working and putting food on the table for you and your mother, you little cry baby, huh? Ever think of that? If you are going to live in his house you live by his rules! God, you and your mother are just sucking him dry! Now close your eyes and remember how his calloused hands felt as they struck your chubby twelve-year-old face.

IN THE FUTURE . . .

Don't watch any more movies with Kevin Costner. Except Waterworld, which was amazing.

WTFACT: The house and farm used in the 1988 movie *Field of Dreams* is located in Dyersville, Iowa, and is still there for tourists to come and play on the field. No ghost sighting has ever been reported.

28. Your favorite expression, "We're not in Kansas anymore," doesn't make as much sense in Wichita.

You love saying "We're not in Kansas" anymore. What a classic line from such a classic film, your childhood favorite: *The Wizard of Oz*. You say it whenever you can. It's one of the sayings that makes you who you are. But now that you are in Kansas, it's doesn't make any sense. What now?

The WTF Approach to Sayings That Don't Make Any F*#!-ing Sense

➤ OPTION #1

Stop being lame. Stop being a total fucking geek and lose the expression. You're a grown man for Christ's sake. And you wonder why you can't get laid. Come up with an alternative, hipper version of the expression, something that also denotes a feeling of being outside a comfortable and familiar place. Substitute "Kansas" for something more gangsta. "Looks like we aren't in the South Bronx anymore"—something like that.

➤ OPTION #2

Say it anyway. Don't let people change you. If you are the kind of nerd that uses expressions like "We're not in Kansas anymore" than be that nerd and be proud of it. Maybe using the expression in Kansas is even more ironic.

➤ OPTION #3

Get a dog and name it Toto. Go all the way with this thing. Balls to the wall. Get a dog named Toto, start dressing like Dorothy, and click your heels every time some corn-fed redneck calls you a fag.

➤ KANSAS'S FINEST

TOP FIVE FILMS THAT TAKE PLACE IN THE GREAT STATE OF KANSAS

1. *In Cold Blood* (1967)
2. *The Wizard of Oz* (1939)
3. *Twister* (1996)
4. *The Walls of Jericho* (1948)
5. *Kansas* (1988)

FAMOUS PEOPLE FROM KANSAS

1. Annette Bening—actress
2. Ed Asner—actor
3. Faya Dynamite—model and stripper voted 2010's "GGurls Booty of the Year"

29. Everything is not up to date in Kansas City.

You've always wanted to go to Kansas City, Missouri. A huge Rogers and Hammerstein fan, you grew up hearing musicals like *Oklahoma!* Although "The Surrey with the Fringe on Top" and "Oh, What a Beautiful Mornin'" get all the attention, your favorite jingle was the upbeat "Everything Is Up to Date in Kansas City." If that was true in the mid-nineteenth century, you reasoned, it must be true today. Finally, you can take a vacation, and off to Kansas City you go, expecting to see the culture capital of the world, a city on the cutting edge in every way. Whoops. Welcome to Kansas City.

The WTF Approach to F*#!-ing Being Stuck in Kansas City

➤ OPTION #1

Try Kansas City, Kansas. Go to the Kansas side of Kansas City. Maybe that is where all the action and excitement is. When you get there turn back and go to Option #2.

➤ OPTION #2

Bring it up to date. Bring Kansas City into the twenty-first century. Or even the twentieth. Start with the twentieth. You don't want to get burned out too quickly.

➤ OPTION #3

Enjoy your stay. Kansas City has a lot to offer. There is the great Gateway Arch, standing 360 feet tall, a glorious tribute to the Westward expansion of the nineteenth century. Oh, that's in St. Louis? WTF?

➤ OPTION #4

Eat some BBQ. Okay, so maybe everything isn't up to date in Kansas City. You won't find bullet trains like in Tokyo or avant-garde theater like in New York City. But you will find some of the best barbecue in the world. Pig out, take a nap, and fly back home.

➤ OPTION #5

Write a new song. Shit, write a new musical that properly represents Kanas City today. Sure it will probably be boring as hell, but at least it will be accurate. Then take it to Broadway baby and become a famous writer.

WTFACT: Kansas City has more boulevards than Paris and more fountains than any other city in the world—except for Rome.

WTFACT: The above fact does not make Kansas City worth visiting.

30. You accidentally light the biggest ball of yarn on fire.

Making your way across the country, you stop at some of America's national treasures. The Lincoln Memorial in Washington, D.C., Mount Rushmore in South Dakota, and of course, the biggest ball of twine in Cawker City, Kansas. So there it is, the biggest ball of yarn in the world. Wow. Who ever thought that it would be so big and so, you know, spherical, you think to yourself as you take the last drag off your cigarette and toss it to the ground. Oops. You didn't think Kansas was known for its windy climate but before you know it, the biggest ball of yarn is quite quickly becoming the biggest fucking fire you've ever seen.

The WTF Approach to Dealing with a F*#!-ing Twine Ball Fire

> **OPTION #1**

Grab a hose. Hopefully Farmer Frank also has the world's biggest hose as well. No, not like that. Don't be a pervert.

> **OPTION #2**

Use Frank's tears. Poor Frank, watching his life's work (unquestionably stupid and pointless as it is) going up in flames. Use his tears to put out the fire and save what's left of his beloved ball of twine.

➤ OPTION #3

Fly the flag at half-mast. This is a national tragedy, and the country needs time to mourn. Fly the flag at half-mast and remember that heroes come in all forms. Some fight for their country and selflessly sacrifice for the greater good, and some sit in a barn and roll fuckin' twine.

➤ OPTION #4

Make another one. You know the saying, you break it, you buy it. Well in this case, you burn, you rebuild it. Get rolling. Sure it might take you years to do it, but this time you can use fire-retardant yarn.

In 1953, Frank Stoeber, like many of his farmer friends, had twine to spare. He decided to roll spare bits of sisal twine into a small ball in his barn to keep things tidy. But instead of disposing of the twine, Frank kept on rolling. In 1961, Stoeber had over 1,600,000 feet of twine rolled into a sphere 11 feet in diameter. Graciously, he gave the twine ball over to the town of Cawker City, Kansas.

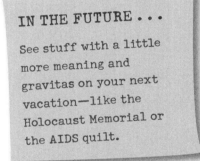

IN THE FUTURE . . .

See stuff with a little more meaning and gravitas on your next vacation—like the Holocaust Memorial or the AIDS quilt.

for the ladies . . .

Start crying and blame the whole incident on the fact that you are on your period.

31. You get arrested for flashing in the "Show-Me" state.

Missourians like to think of themselves as stalwart, skeptical characters. The kind of folk that don't just buy whatever it is you're selling just because you sound good selling it. That's right. This is what the whole "Show–Me" state thing is supposed to mean. It doesn't—we repeat: it doesn't—mean that you show your cock in the middle of downtown St. Louis on a bright sunny day. Seriously, put it away, already!

The WTF Approach to Defending Your F*#!-ing Flashing Ways

➤ OPTION #1

Show the jury. Not your dick. Show them how easy it is to misunderstand the meaning of such an ambiguous motto as the "Show-Me" state. Seriously. What else could it mean to a new resident like yourself? Make sure to sound real folksy and mention the Bible if you can somehow. They love that book there.

➤ OPTION #2

Show them . . . the money. You can get out of any sticky situation with cash. Money talks, bullshit walks. Then again, showing your cock on the street is the kind of bullshit that might get you into trouble that even money can't help you talk your way out of.

➤ OPTION #3

Show them again. Hey. Maybe they didn't get a good look. If you are showing your penis everywhere around town, it's probably something pretty special. Let the judge and jury take a real close look at it.

➤ OPTION #4

Flip the switch. Act horrified every time you see someone's ankles. Start yelling about how offensive it is that people are exposing their bare ankles in public. Then start suing people for the pain and anguish that you have endured.

for the ladies . . .

Save your Vajajay for someone special—like the guy in the bar whose name you don't remember but you think it started with a "J" like John. Or was it a "P" like Paul? Anyway, yeah, him.

IN THE FUTURE . . .

When in doubt, don't take off your pants unless you are alone with a girl or a doctor. Please.

SHOW ME THE MISSOURI

Legend has it that the "Show-Me" state motto was coined when Missouri Congressman Willard Duncan Vandiver declared at an 1899 naval banquet in Philadelphia: "I come from a state that raises corn and cotton and cockleburs and Democrats, and frothy eloquence neither convinces nor satisfies me. I am from Missouri. You have got to show me."

32. A twister is coming and you can't find the key to your tornado shelter.

Oh shit, here comes another one. Luckily you're a veteran midwesterner. This ain't your first rodeo. Heck, you've survived more tornadoes than Lindsay Lohan has survived drug overdoses. So when the winds start picking up you calmly head down to your shelter. But when you get there you realize that the key is not on the hook. What?! How can that be? You frantically search, but it's nowhere to be found. The twister is closing in. You can hear the trees being pulled from the ground. Uh-oh.

The WTF Approach to Dealing with a F*#!-ing Twister

> **OPTION #1**

Pinch yourself. Maybe this is a just a bad dream? A nightmare. Like the one you always have about being naked in class with an erection and everyone laughing and mocking you.

> **OPTION #2**

Grab your skateboard and a video camera. This is going to be the most awesome skateboarding video ever. Goodbye anonymity, hello YouTube fame.

➤ OPTION #3

Find Toto. You don't want to be in a foreign land without your little doggy now, do you? LOL. You have a dog named, Toto? Ha ha.

➤ OPTION #4

Repent your sins. Obviously you are being punished by God for your lascivious lifestyle. Repent and pray that God's wrath skips over your homestead just like he skipped over the homes of the Jews as he killed Egyptian babies. If you do happen to have an Egyptian baby, then you should have seen this coming, asshole.

➤ OPTION #5

Go to your neighbor's house. Shit, everyone has a tornado shelter; just crash in on someone else's. Then again, your nearest neighbor is probably twenty miles away; on second thought kiss your ass goodbye.

> **WTFACT:** Tornadoes occur mostly between 3 and 9 P.M. The average tornado moves from southwest to northeast. The average forward speed is 30 mph, but may vary from nearly stationary to 70 mph. ~www.infoplease.com

WTF: UP CLOSE AND PERSONAL

"My girlfriend and I were having sex one day at my parent's house when a twister hit. We were right in the middle when my girlfriend started screaming. I just thought I was doing really well, then she pushed me off and headed for the door. When I realized what was happening I followed her. We headed down into the shelter where my mom and younger sister were. She started yelling at me. Apparently I ran out so quick I forget to put my pants on. Still to this day when it's windy I get a hard-on."

—Craig Verdoes, Kansas City Tornado Survivor and Sex Addict

TORNADOES ARE NO LAUGHING MATTER

Q: What do a tornado and a redneck divorce have in common?
A: In the end, someone is going to lose a house trailer.

Q: What do hot girls and tornados have in common?
A: In the beginning, there's a lot of sucking and blowing. Then afterward, they take your house.

WHICH IS WORSE? TORNADOES OR HURRICANES?

Tornadoes	Hurricanes
Very strong winds	Intense energy and wind
Cover a smaller area	Can cause widespread damage
Last a short time	Can last a few hours
Took Dorothy to Oz	Yet to have a great movie about one

chapter four

don't mess with texas

33. You messed with Texas.

Everything is bigger in Texas. The people, the hats, and the Death Row wing in prison. Texans love to kill criminals; they love to right the wrongs and bring down the impartial hammer of justice. "Don't Mess with Texas," is the motto. In other words, you just committed murder in the wrong state, partner.

The WTF Approach to Getting Out of F*#!-ing Texas Alive

➤ OPTION #1

Bring the victim back to life. Hey, God brought Lazarus back. Why can't you bring back Joanne? Give it a shot, dummy.

➤ OPTION #2

Say the victim was a liberal. In Texas, murder will get you the death penalty. However, if you kill a liberal you only get five years—it's considered a community service.

➤ OPTION #3

Self-defense. Texans take property rights pretty damn seriously. If someone crosses your property line at the old homestead, you can shoot him in the face and bury him in the backyard.

➤ OPTION #4

Call Susan Sarandon. In *Dead Man Walking*, she really helped out Sean Penn. Sure he was executed anyway, but his soul was unburdened by the end.

➤ OPTION #5

Start looking at menus. Hey, the last meal is all you have to look forward to. Should you go with what you know you like or should you try something different, like Indian food. Indian food always gives you gas afterward. Oh that's right that won't matter because you'll be fuckin' dead.

MATCHING GAME

Match the number of executions in 2012 with the corresponding state:

1.	Texas	A.	3
2.	California	B.	17
3.	Ohio	C.	0
4.	Florida	D.	1
5.	Wyoming	E.	8

Answers: Texas B, California A, Ohio E, Florida C, Wyoming D

34. You're invited to dinner in Dallas, but you're allergic to BBQ sauce.

Texans love three things above all else in this order: barbecue, Jesus, and executing innocent prisoners. Yes sir, nothing gets a cowboy hungrier than the smell of that sweet, smoky barbecue sauce. Yee haw! Now, that's a tasty Texan treat. Unfortunately, however—like Jesus and executing the potentially innocent—you don't get all hot and giggly about barbecue sauce. In fact, you can't even eat the damned stuff. What to do when you're allergic to BBQ in cowboy country?

The WTF Approach to Dealing with a F*#!-ing BBQ Allergy

➤ OPTION #1

Cowboy up. Listen, partner. You want to hang with the big boys in the big state of Texas? You're going to have to get tough. That means wearing tight jeans, patterned shirts, and big buckles with your name on them (so diva!). It also means

being able to suck down three or four hundred BBQ ribs at a sitting. So cowboy up and deal with the sickness later.

➤ OPTION #2

Move to Arkansas. They used to call the state the "poor man's Texas." Maybe they're so broke there they can't afford barbecue sauce. Check it out.

➤ OPTION #3

BYO dinner. Bring a tofu salad or whatever your bitch ass likes to eat. Sure you'll get plenty of stares and head shakes, but it's better than dying. Then again, you do live in Texas, so you might've died and gone to hell already.

➤ OPTION #4

Enter a pie-eating contest, or any other stuffing-your-face related activity to earn your respect as a big eater and a bigger man.

Shove down a 75-ounce rib eye instead. You'll get mad respect.

BBQ HISTORY

There seems to be evidence that the ingenious peoples of North and South America taught the Europeans (who mostly grilled) how to barbecue by cooking their meat slowly over a long period of time. But it was the European settlers (mostly of German stock) in South Carolina who seem to have developed that delicious sauce.

FOUR FOOD GROUPS

There are four kinds of BBQ sauce, each using a varying degree of these ingredients:

1. Vinegar and pepper
2. Mustard
3. Light tomato
4. Heavy tomato

35. You booked a vacation to Paris, Texas.

After a few beers and some shopping around online for cheap flights, you've decided to go on vacation. Hell, you deserve it. Fueled by your beers, you decide to go book a trip and decide on Paris. Ah Paris . . . wine, croissants, French women; this will be a trip to remember. You even order Rosetta Stone so you can learn enough French to get laid. By the next morning you suddenly realize in your drunken state you have made a horrible mistake you're not going to Paris, France, turns out you booked a nonrefundable flight to Paris, Texas. WTF?

The WTF Approach to F*#!-ing Up Your Vacation

➤ OPTION #1

C'est la vie. Hey if everything happens for a reason, this might be the perfect trip for you. You can still learn French and then pretend to be from France. Chicks love French men. You'll probably end up getting way more ass this way.

➤ OPTION #2

Fight it. Call the airline and explain the situation—in English. They probably won't refund your money, but maybe they might give you credit for another flight. Next time, don't book your flight when you're drunk, asshole.

> ► OPTION #3

Gift it. Give it away to someone you really don't like but need to be nice to—like your in-laws. They will think you're the sweetest guy—until they see it's Texas, not France. Then they'll go right back to wishing you were dead.

WTFACT: Did you know Paris, Texas, also has an Eiffel Tower? In fact, it's their number one attraction and stands sixty-five feet tall. While it's not the biggest Eiffel Tower replica in the United States, it is the only one to have a giant red cowboy hat perched on it. In 1995, the Paris Eiffel Tower earned the title of Best Pit Stop by the Great North American Race. Wow! What an accomplishment. So bring a camera—and a gun to shoot yourself after.

DUPLICATE CITY NAMES IN OTHER STATES

Hollywood, CA	Hollywood, FL
Las Vegas, NV	Las Vegas, NM
Dallas, GA	Dallas, TX
New Castle, VA	New Castle, DE
Glendale, CA	Glendale, AZ
Salem, VA	Salem, OR
Buena Vista, CO	Buena Vista, VA
Springfield	Just About Everywhere

36. You live in Texas but can't stand high school football.

Texas is state known for its BBQ, cowboys, and racially insensitive ranches. Everything's bigger in Texas goes the saying—high school football especially. Texans eat, sleep, and breathe high school football. That's all you ever hear about. At work, at the bar, and the gas station. "Did you catch the game?' It seems that in Texas more people attend a high school football game than church. The only problem is that you can't stand football—and Jesus hates you for it.

The WTF Approach to Surviving F*#!-ing High School Football

➤ OPTION #1

Focus on the cheerleaders. If you don't like the game, certainly you can stomach the sight of young high school cheerleaders bouncing up and down screaming their heads off. If you can't, then get the hell out of Texas—pronto.

➤ OPTION #2

Stick to your guns, literally. Carry a gun at all times and the next time some asshole Texan says "You don't like high school football?! What are you, a pussy?" show him who the pussy is by taking his life.

➤ OPTION #3

Adopt a really athletic poor kid. Look, it worked for Sandra Bullock in *The Blind Side*. Go out and find a really big kid with no money and adopt him. Send him to school and force him to play football. Then he will get drafted and make millions, which of course he will share with his "Daddy." See? Football is fun—and profitable.

for the ladies . . .

Who gives a shit if you like football? You don't have to like the game, just wear the jersey, guys love that shit. Make sure to tie it so everyone can see your belly button ring. Slut.

WTF: UP CLOSE AND PERSONAL

"I will like any game that gives me the best odds of getting laid."
—Jodi Miller, coauthor of WTF

"Nobody in football should be called a genius. A genius is a guy like Norman Einstein."

—Joe Theismann

WTF ADVICE: HOW TO FAKE LIKE YOU'RE A REAL MAN

You don't have to be a football fan to talk shop with some bozo at the water cooler about the game. Two words: distract and deflect.

Joe Football: Hey did you catch the game last night?

You: Do I look like a homosexual?

Joe Football: Ha. Yeah, great game. Miller at the 50 yard line. Was that something or what?

You: Unbelievable. I was just thinking the same thing.

Joe Football: You think they're gonna go all the way?

You: Is the sky fucking blue?

Joe Football: So funny. I didn't know if you were into football, who's your team?

You: Who's my team? Come on buddy, who the fuck else?

Joe Football: I don't know, who?

You: What?

Joe Football: Who's your team?

You: Did you see Angela today in Marketing with the cleavage?

Joe Football: Do I look like a homosexual?

> "When I went to Catholic high school in Philadelphia, we just had one coach for football and basketball. He took all of us who turned out and had us run through a forest. The ones who ran into the trees were on the football team."
>
> —George Raveling

37. Everything is bigger in Texas—except your penis.

At first you were optimistic. Surely it would grow once you hit puberty. So what if you were smaller than everyone else in the locker room. By the time you hit high school you reckon that your penis would be the pride of Texas. But that never came to pass. You're like a Texas expression "all hat and no cattle" or, more specifically, "all balls and no dick." WTF?

The WTF Approach to Living in Texas with a Little F*#!-ing Penis

➤ OPTION #1

Make a lot of money in oil. Even today there is a lot of money to be made in oil and gas in Texas. Start a claim and hit it big. Remember, the only thing women love more than a guy with a big cock is a guy with a lot of money.

➤ OPTION #2

Blame your father. Most dudes get their penis from their father. Track him down and challenge him to a gunfight. Sure a pissing contest would be less dangerous, but no one in the town square wants to look at your little dicks fighting it out.

➤ OPTION #3

Make it bigger. Go out and buy a penis pump, or better yet, get a penile implant. Look, if the ladies can make their tits bigger with surgery, why can't you do the same with your johnson? Sure there's a small chance of the surgery going horribly wrong and your penis never getting erect again, but aren't you willing to take that chance? Ya gotta play big to win big!

> **WTFACT:** In an online study of 25,000 men, over 50 percent said they were unhappy with the size of their penis.

for the ladies …

If you have a penis, you're not really a lady.

> **WTFACT:** The male penis typically stops growing in size by age fifteen. Remember that when you hear of a female school teacher taking advantage of a "child" in class. His mind may be immature, but his pee-pee is fully grown.

WTF: UP CLOSE AND PERSONAL

I do not like my penis. I am getting a penile implant and filming it in a documentary called *Big Like Me: One Man's Quest to Enlarge His Penis*. It is a remarkable film of one man's journey to do whatever it takes to be happy and big. Coming soon to a theater near you!

—GB

38. Your fellow Texans decide to secede from the Union.

It's finally happening! After threatening on Fox News several times, your state of Texas has finally decided to secede from the United States. You can't wait to bring the Texas Republic back to its glory days, when Texans could decide their own future, determine your own destiny. But despite all this excitement, you're a little concerned that the United States might not go along with this. And if you thought the last time Texas seceded was an uphill battle, wait until the drones start coming. Uh-oh.

The WTF Approach to Dealing with a Pissed-Off F*#!-ing Union

➤ OPTION #1

Head to the Alamo. This is where the last showdown went down between the Republic of Texas and those who tried to steal their freedom. Face north this time though, since the Mexicans won't be the ones you'll have to contend with.

➤ OPTION #2

Get other Southern states to join the fight. Everyone in the South speaks about the "War of Northern Aggression" like it was yesterday. Deep down, most Southerners want a second chance to beat the Yankees to a pulp once and for all. Start the Civil War all over again and see if this time is different.

➤ OPTION #3

Start up the Underground Railroad again. Chances are the minute the secession takes place the powers that be will reinstitute slavery, most likely importing slaves from Mexico this time around. Be a hero and send these Mexican slaves north to the promised land, where they can toil with the rest of us.

WTF RANT

WTF is up with the South saying the Civil War was about defending our way of life? That's sometimes what you hear from Southerners sympathetic to the South's cause in the Civil War. True, the South did fight to defend their way of life. Unfortunately, for over a quarter of the population, that way of life depended on them to work for free as property, not people. Basically, your way of life fucking sucked.

chapter five

east coast shuffle

39. You live in NYC and are petrified of crowds.

New York. The Big Apple. The City That Never Sleeps. Gotham. You love New York. You love the food. You love the culture. But there is one thing about the city that you can't stand—all the friggin' people! What to do when you love New York City but can't stand crowds?

The WTF Approach to Overcoming Your F*#!-ing Fear of Crowds

➤ OPTION #1

Time your plans carefully. Even the city that never sleeps takes a nap. Hang out from about 4:30 A.M. to about 6 A.M. on the weekdays. It won't be dead, but there won't be big crowds either. Only hookers and homeless are out at those times. You'll fit right in.

➤ OPTION #2

Become a hermit. In this day and age there is really no need to ever leave your apartment. Set up an office and work from home. If you

become a really disgusting hermit and start hoarding shit, you might even get to be on a reality show about agoraphobic hoarders. Awesome!

➤ OPTION #3

Conquer your fears. Get over it already. Immerse yourself in the crowds at Grand Central during rush hour and learn to get over your fears. You might even begin to draw strength from them. Think of Bruce Wayne's fear of bats in *Batman Begins.* So, you want to be a superhero or you want to be a pussy? Make your choice, putz.

STEPS TO TAKE IN A RIOT OR STAMPEDE

- Look for an exit.
- Find a higher ground to stand on.
- Stick close to another person.
- Scream like the little pussy you really are.
- Use another person as a human shield and save yourself!

WTF RANT

What the fuck is up with flash mobs? When did jumping up and surprising someone with song and dance become acceptable? Or entertaining. And why the fuck doesn't Howie Mandel ever say no to a show?

40. You drop a penny off the Empire State Building and kill someone.

New York City: there are many sites to see. Times Square, The Museum of Modern Art, the hookers at Hunt's Point. But nothing compares to the great Empire State Building. After waiting in line for a few days you finally get to the top and marvel at the view. The city is so peaceful from above. Plus, you can't smell the urine on the street. You decide to make a wish. You reach for a penny and chuck it off the edge. Suddenly you hear people below start screaming. You look down and see a crowd of people standing over some dude; turns out that penny gained a lot speed on the way down and hit this guy on the head killing him instantly. Oh shit, you came to New York . . . took in the sights . . . and killed someone. Whoops.

The WTF Approach to Getting Away with F*#!-ing Murder

➤ OPTION #1

Forgettaboutit. Hey, the fuckin' piece of shit should have been paying attention. What is he fuckin' stoopid?

➤ OPTION #2

Play dumb. Act as surprised as everyone else. Say things like "What a shame," "Poor guy," and "Who would do this?" Then while everyone else is lamenting over this unfortunate schmuck, get the hell out of there. Take the stairs. No one will find you there.

➤ OPTION #3

Blame the terrorists. Why not? They deserve it, right? Start yelling about terrorists coming to New York and killing people with pocket change. Start a protest and soon you'll get the government taking notice. Propose a law that no one can carry change anymore. Extreme, maybe, but we're sure the guy you killed would approve.

➤ OPTION #4

Confess. But not to the police— just to Jesus Christ, right before you die. This way you stay out of jail but still secure everlasting life in God's Kingdom! A win-win for everyone . . . except the guy with the hole in his friggin' head down below.

WTF: FASTER THAN A SPEEDING BULLET?

If you drop a penny off of the Empire State Building, it can travel up to a 100 miles per hour. If you masturbate off the edge, your semen can travel up to 250 miles per hour. Imagine a facial that would actually remove a face? Awesome! Here are some other objects and their maximum speeds to consider:

Penny: 100 mph
Quarter: 175 mph
Nut: 250 mph
Cell Phone: 500 mph

41. Someone cuts down the tree you watched grow from your Brooklyn window.

It's hard coming of age. The ups and downs of childhood and adolescence. The one thing that was always constant in your life was your tree. The tree you planted when you were just a boy. The tree you tied a tire swing to and spent hours playing on. The tree you climbed up to look into the windows of teenage girls while they undressed. Your tree, you love it so. But then one morning out of the blue you hear a sound you could swear is a chainsaw. You get up to see what's going on, only to see some strange man cutting down your tree. WHAT!!!! Not your tree! NOOOOOOOOO!

The WTF Guide to Dealing with the Loss of Your F*#!-ing Childhood Tree

➤ OPTION #1

Have a funeral. Invite friends and family to come and celebrate the life of this special tree. Sure people will think you're crazy for having a funeral for a tree but if you serve food and alcohol people will come.

➤ OPTION #2

An eye for an eye. Go outside and take away something from this guy that he has had since his childhood, like his legs. Cut them off and see how he likes it, asshole.

➤ OPTION #3

Plant another one. Go out and buy another tree and grow it. Sure you'll miss the tree that you once climbed up. But now you can nurture a brand new tree. This time maybe get an apple tree so you have something to eat while you peep into women's bedrooms.

➤ OPTION #4

Have a bonfire. That tree belongs to you, so they should give it to you. Cut it up, light it on fire, and have a huge party.

WTFACT: Many believe that the famous story about George Washington cutting down a cherry tree was just that, a story. It was only to illustrate his honesty. That's an interesting way to teach us honesty by telling the country a lie. BTW, what kind of a monster cuts down a cherry tree?

42. You're the only one in your town in New Jersey not on a reality show.

Seems you can't go to a bakery or hair salon without tripping over a reality camera crew filming the next big star. You have the hair, you have the tan, you're lacking basic brain functionality. You have it all. Yet for some reason you're the only guy in your New Jersey town not on a reality show. You go to the auditions and act like an asshole, but you still don't get the part. WTF?

The WTF Approach to Getting Your Own F*#!-ing Reality Show

> **STEP 1**

Create a nickname. Maybe it's not you; it's your name. You need something catchy like "The Situation" or "Snookie." Then start referring to yourself in the third person. That shit will catch on soon, Mr. "Douchenator."

> **STEP 2**

GTL. Maybe you need a little more of the Holy Trinity as dictated by the cast of *The Jersey Shore*. Remember you are competing against millions of other tanned, greasy gym rats in Ed Hardy shirts, so make sure that you take your GTL (gym, tan, laundry) very,

very seriously. Think of it as a job for people who are morons.

> **STEP 3**

Get a following. Get yourself some meat heads and guidettes to follow you around for a while. Pay them in Red Bulls and vodka if you have to. When people see you and your entourage they will start to believe you got something going on to have these idiots following you. Fake it till you make it baby.

> **STEP 4**

Tape it. Start bringing your camera everywhere. The gym, the beach, the bars—your parole hearing. Start getting into fights and make sure you get it all on tape. Don't forget to get the hot tub clip; you'll be a star in no time.

> **STEP 5**

Write a book. All the reality stars have one, even Snookie—and she can barely read. Come up with a catchy title like "I Was a Teenage Douche Bag" or "WTF Reality Stars."

HIP NEW JERSEY

- Jersey Shore
- Jerseylious
- Cake Boss
- Real Housewives of New Jersey

THINGS YOU NEED TO BE ON A REALITY SHOW.

1. A shitty attitude
2. An inflated ego
3. Big tits (or pecs)
4. A lot of money
5. Alcohol or drug problem
6. A litter of kids (six or more)
7. A really tacky house packed with a bunch of shit

43. You can't catch a cab in NYC for the life of you.

Driving in New York City is a pain in the ass. Luckily it's one of the few places in the United States with a real transportation system and plenty of taxis that can take you anywhere you want to go—except certain neighborhoods of course. But you have a problem: you can't seem to ever hail a cab whenever you visit the Big Apple. WTF?

The WTF Approach to Hailing a F*#!-ing Cab in NYC

> ### ➤ OPTION #1

Be white. Talk to any black man in New York and he'll tell you that catching a cab isn't as easy as it looks.

> ### ➤ OPTION #2

Stop whistling. Unless you have one of those really cool whistles that you can hear from blocks away, give up and try sticking out your hand.

> ### ➤ OPTION #3

Get aggressive. Don't let some old woman take the cab just because she's old and has a vagina. Push her out of the way if you need to and get that fuckin' cab. Hey, what're you looking at, old broad? You snooze you lose, bitch. Then start bossing around the cab driver and kvetching that he isn't taking the fastest route to your destination even if secretly you know he is.

➤ OPTION #4

Steal a cab. Why hail a cab when you can own a cab, and by own we mean take for free. Wait until a cabbie pulls over to take a crap then break in and steal that shit. Then start picking up people and make some cash, you'll need it to bail your ass out of jail when you get caught for stealing that cab.

for the ladies . . .

Make yourself more attractive. Only an ugly girl can't hail a cab.

WTF IS UP WITH EVERY CAB DRIVER BEING A BIG SHOT IN HIS HOMELAND?

Every cab driver sings the same tune: "In my country I was engineer of space program, but I moved here with family to wipe semen off back seats in cabs." Really? Sure it's the case sometimes, but it seems unbelievable that every cab driver was a genius in his native land. You never hear a cabby say "In my country I drove a cab. Here, I drive a cab." Never happens. It's like past lives. Everyone was Cleopatra or King Arthur in their past life; no one was a cobbler or a hooker. Seems unlikely. And if the taxi drivers in this country were all big shots in their native land, then who drives the cabs in the shitty countries? Engineers from even shittier countries?

44. You marry into the Mob.

When your first met Angela, you were head over heels in love. She was the perfect combination of sexy and cute. Plus, she was into anal. You even liked her family. They were so friendly and fun—not to mention rich. Who would have thought that sanitation business paid millions? You asked her to be your wife and she accepted. You were in the family now. Life was good. Yet as time went on you began to notice things about this family—different little things that made this family unique. Like the fact that every other week there was either a marriage or a funeral—sometimes the groom would be married and then buried on the same day. Weird. But still you gave them the benefit of the doubt. Surely the mafia was only in movies, nowadays. Then your brother-in-law asked you to hide a body one day and everything suddenly made sense. Shit. Looks like this family has just made you an offer you can't refuse.

The WTF Approach to Life in the F*#!-ing "Family Business"

➤ OPTION #1

Research. Netflix all the seasons of *The Sopranos* and brush up on your knowledge of the Mob. Make sure to practice saying "forgettaboutit" as one word instead of "forget about it." You want to fit in.

➤ OPTION #2

Embrace it. Hey it could be worse. In this economy, just be glad that you're in a family who goes to work at all—even if it involves killing people.

➤ OPTION #3

Become a rat. Call in the FBI and take down the family—Donnie Brasco style. Sure you'll be putting your life at risk, but it's the right thing to do. Then you can go into witness protection and start a new life—in Norway.

➤ OPTION #4

Start a reality show. Shit, they have *Mob Wives*, why not *Mob Husbands*? Start taping your life with this family and sell the show to Bravo—they'll buy any show that involves scumbags.

MAFIA MATCHING GAME

Match the famous gangster to his "family."

1. Boss: Joseph Massino
2. Boss: Carmine "Junior" Persico
3. Boss: Vincent "Chin" Gigante
4. Boss: Buddy Valastro

A. Bananno
B. Cake boss family
C. Colombo
D. Genovese

Answers: 1. A; 2. C; 3. D; 4. B

45. You get harassed at a Boston Red Sox game for rooting for the other team.

First of all, you are a moron. Sorry, but if you had read the chapter on Boston in any travel book, you would know that Bostonians care about three things and not in this order: Revolutionary War history, the romanticization of the lobsterman, and local sports teams.

A Harvard study showed that the chances of a New England–born Red Sox fanatic surviving a night out at an Irish Pub next to Fenway is about 50 percent. Now, if you are rooting for the other team, the chances of survival decrease by a factor of ten. If you are a Yankee fan, fuhgeddaboudit. Call the cops before you land at Logan. Not that they'll be any help.

The WTF Approach to Escaping the Beantown Beat Down

> **OPTION #1**

Convert. Fuck your team and your hometown. First of all, how many of the players on the team are even from your hometown? Even from your country? What exactly engenders this kind of perverse loyalty? Well, whatever it is just convert to the Boston teams. New Englanders are provincial, fierce regionalists, and not super-accepting or friendly to outsiders. BUT, they accept anyone who loves what they love: multicolored leaves slowly falling from trees in the autumn breeze and Tom Brady's tight ass. Join the party, or there is no party in Boston for you.

> **OPTION #2**

Run and don't look back. Run for your life. Irish-descended Bostonians are good boxers, but how many have ever won a marathon lately? Leave and never come back. Make sure to take the Duck Tour first; it's actually pretty cool. To inspire you, remember what women look like outside of Boston. Imagine running to a place where wearing a brand new oversized Patriots sweatshirt isn't considered "dressing up." That should inspire you, no matter where you live. If you must, wear a disguise so your enemies don't recognize you.

> **OPTION #3**

Fight them. Stand for yourself and "your" team, even though the only thing you own of your team is a hat. True, team loyalty is a pointless and meaningless thing to fight for, but your life is pretty pointless overall, isn't it?

Next time show up with a really hot chick. They might still harass you, but chances are they'll attack her instead.

for the ladies . . .

Show them your tits. This will stop any guy in his tracks, at least for a second then your boyfriend can sucker punch and game over.

WTFACT: Massachusetts has the best public education system in the country.

WTFACT: More people in Massachusetts read newspapers and go to college than in any other state per capita.

WTFACT: We included these flattering facts strictly to avoid being beaten to death by a brazen Bostonian the next time we're in Beantown.

WTF RANT

It's just a game! We all know these guys. The overweight accountant that plays short stop for the office co-ed softball league. He constantly screams things like "Come on!!! You have to dive for that!!" Or "Get your head in the game and out of your ass!" WTF is up with this tool? And by the way, if you don't find this funny, then *you're* that guy, asshole! To all of those guys out there, newsflash: no one is coming to recruit you. You're not getting the call to go to the "show." You're playing with all the other out-of-shape losers from your office that after the game are going to ice their sore muscles and plan the next office birthday party. Our advice, chill the fuck out!

46. You live in Philadelphia and you hate Rocky.

Philadelphia is mostly known as the City of Brotherly Love, the city of the cheesesteak, and the city where Tom Hanks died of AIDS. Also synonymous with Philadelphia is *Rocky*, an epic American film that chronicles the rise of an unknown boxer as he takes on the world champion. Who can forget the iconic shot of Sylvester Stallone on the steps of the Art Museum overlooking downtown Philadelphia, his arms raised, ready to take on the world? Well, apparently you can. Because despite being a born and bred Philly boy you feel the same way about that movie as a vegetarian does about a cheesesteak—disgust. WTF?

The WTF Approach to Avoiding the "Italian Stallion"

➤ OPTION #1

Like other Philadelphia-based movies. Maybe your friends and family will forgive your dislike of *Rocky* if you like other Philly films. Here are some of Philly's finest. Try *Philadelphia*, *The Sixth Sense*, *Trading Places*, *Witness*, and if you can stomach Nicholas Cage—*The Dawn of the Dead*.

➤ OPTION #2

Become Rocky. If you don't like *Rocky* because you found it too unrealistic, become a down-and-out boxer and make your way ringside in Vegas, face to face with the champ. Make sure to find a mildly attractive woman with a fat, piggish brother to fall head over heels in love with.

➤ OPTION #3

Bring cheesesteaks and wear your Eagles jersey. If you wear your Eagles jersey with pride to every social function and bring a bag full of cheesesteaks, every Philly friend might forgive your blasphemy about the famous boxing film.

for the ladies . . .

You don't have to like *Rocky* to be popular. You just have to put out.

MATCHING GAME

Match the city to the movie's location

1. *Escape from New York*
2. *Jersey Girl*
3. *Chinatown*
4. *Leaving Las Vegas*
5. *Mr. Smith Goes to Washington*

A. Washington, D.C.
B. Las Vegas
C. New York
D. New Jersey
E. Chinatown

Answers: If you seriously thought about any of these, you've obviously been hit in the head as many times as Rocky.

47. You're a Pennsylvania Quaker but you can't stand Quaker Oats.

Some say there is more to being a Quaker than eating Quaker Oats. A lot more. But your father was very strict about eating your oatmeal every morning. "Thou shan't ever start the day without filling thy belly with those delightful Quaker Oats."Yes, eating that particular brand of oatmeal every morning was sacrosanct. A religious and spiritual obligation. But you hated it so much that when you grew up you swore it off for good. And then, your whole life mysteriously began to unravel—your health went down the shitter and everything else followed. Turns out father was right, and eating your oats just might be the way to get your life back on track. But you hate it! WTF?

The WTF Approach to Eating Your F*#!-ing Oatmeal

➤ OPTION #1

Hold your nose. Haven't you ever seen *Fear Factor?* Almost anything is edible if you hold your nose shut—except maybe a woman after a long, long run. But you wouldn't know about that would you, Quaker boy?

➤ OPTION #2

Inject it. Blend the oats, put them in a syringe and mainline that bitch.

➤ OPTION #3

Commit suicide. You've already disappointed your father, who is watching your pathetic life in shame. Him and the Quaker Oats guy are appalled and ashamed that you are one of them, a Quaker. If they weren't pacifists they'd come back down to Earth and kick the shit out of you.

WTFACT: Quakers are known for being pacifists. They were also the first religious group in America to vocally denounce slavery.

WTFACT: The term "Quaker" refers to a member of the "Religious Society of Friends." Aw, they even sound nice.

WTF AMERICA QUIZ

Which of the following Quakers did not exactly live up to that whole "pacifist" ideal?

- **A.** William Penn

- **B.** Herbert Hoover

- **C.** James Dean

- **D.** Ben Kingsley

- **E.** Richard Nixon

Answer: E

48. You would rather live as a slave than die—and everyone in your New Hampshire town knows it.

Live Free or Die. That's the New Hampshire state motto, and unquestionably the most gangsta of all the state mottos. It was Revolutionary War hero and distinguished son of New Hampshire General John Stark who first said those powerful word, words that New Hampshire natives still take fucking seriously. But really? Would you really rather die than live free? Ever since you questioned this state maxim in junior high school class one day, the whole town knows that you would rather live a slave than die a free man. Basically, everyone in town knows you're a pussy.

The WTF Approach to Dealing with a F*#!-ing Town That Hates Your Guts

➤ OPTION #1

Live as a slave and see how bad it is. You will probably have a better life than most people. You will have a job, a place to live, and probably some form of health care. Think about it, in this economy freedom is nothing compared to stability. So post an add on Craigslist as a slave looking for a master. You'll get plenty of responses. Trust us.

> **OPTION #2**

Rewrite the state motto. Become a state senator and campaign to change the motto to something more practical, and more fitting of life in contemporary New Hampshire. Here are some potential ones you can feel free to use:

- Live in the woods with a truck and be a lesbian
- Live in a place as beautiful as Vermont but with crazy people
- Live in New Hampshire. Not because you want to, but because you can't afford a house in Massachusetts.

> **OPTION #3**

Make them eat their words. Get a gun (shouldn't be hard in New Hampshire) and force people to be your slave or die. See how many of these big shots change their mind. You'll have the whole state either at your beck and call or six feet under in no time.

IN THE FUTURE . . .

Never show weakness. Girls don't like it.

for the ladies . . .

Once you get married you're technically a slave anyway, right?

SIMILAR MOTTOS THROUGHOUT HISTORY

- 1775 in Virginia: "Give me liberty or give me death!"
- France during the French Revolution: "Liberty, Equality, Brotherhood, or Death"
- British Army: "Better to die than to be a coward"
- E! Entertainment–"Love the Kardashians or die." (We would choose death)

49. After reading too much Stephen King, your small town in Maine scares the shit out of you.

Maine is one of the least populated, most physically beautiful states. The rocky coastline, the wooded forests, the quaint towns along the shimmering sea. Maine has charm leaking out of its fucking ears. There's nothing scary about small-town Maine. Unless, of course, you read a novel by the proud Maine native, Stephen King, whose horror novels take place almost exclusively in those quiet little Maine towns. Halfway through Pet Sematary you begin to look at your town in Maine a little differently. In fact, it scares the fucking shit out of you.

The WTF Approach to Being F*#!-ing Petrified of Your Small Town

➤ **OPTION #1**

Read a nice story that takes place in Maine. Stephen King may write about the murderous Maine, but there are other writers who write about the Maine that you know, the quiet, quaint, peaceful Maine. Check out Nora Roberts. Her romantic tales of love and loss in Maine might make your eyes water, but they won't make you shit your pants.

➤ OPTION #2

Become an animal hoarder. If you are afraid to leave just get a bunch of animals and keep them as your friends/prisoners. Then get on a reality show and make enough money to pay for a one-way ticket out of Murderville, USA, once and for all.

➤ OPTION #3

Become the villain. If you become the kind of murderer that Stephen King writes about, a serial killer hunting down unsuspecting residents of your small town, then you don't have to be scared anymore. Everyone will be scared of you, instead.

WTFACT: It's not his fault that Stephen King writes such scary shit. When he was just a kid, he saw a friend get hit and killed by a train. Then, in 1999, King was hit by a van and almost died. And he's a die-hard Red Sox fan. Now, that's scary shit!

TOP FIVE THINGS TO DO IN MAINE

1. Eat lobster
2. Look at trees from inside a seafood restaurant
3. Look at the ocean and cliffs from inside a seafood restaurant
4. Eat lobster bisque
5. Try not to get raped by drunken lobsterman

chapter six

california dreamin'

50. You live in Hollywood, but you're not in the entertainment business—you're a librarian.

Hundreds of thousands flock to Tinsteltown with big dreams of becoming the next big thing. Mostly, their dreams are crushed slowly under a blanket of sunshine and bad traffic. They turn to drink. They turn to drugs. Some of them are even reduced to whoring themselves out to the book business.

Yep, you can't throw a rock in this city without hitting someone working on their screenplay or rehearsing a script for a pilot. Everyone is in the industry except for you. You are a librarian, for real. You love your job but every time you tell someone what you do, they invariably ask "a librarian? And what else?" Nothing. You have no desire to be in the entertainment business; in fact you don't even own a TV. You read . . . a lot.

The WTF Approach to Being a F*#!-ing Librarian in Hollywood

➤ OPTION #1

Be proud. Hey in a town of wannabes you really stick out. Sure, as a nerdy loser, but still. At least you're original. And be thankful that you have a steady paycheck, unlike most actors. Well, for now anyway, but once e-books completely take over the world you'll be obsolete, an out of work librarian living in the city of dreams. How poetic. Hmm, might make for a great show?

➤ OPTION #2

Take some classes. Come on, deep down inside you know you have the acting bug, everyone does. And even if you really don't, it might be good to take an acting class, get you out of your shell and teach you to be more social and outgoing at parties. Just kidding. You're a librarian! You don't go to parties.

➤ OPTION #3

Flip the switch. When people ask you what you do tell them "You moved out to Hollywood to become a librarian" Watch as the fame-fixated actors struggle to figure out just what you mean by that.

At least you're doing something you love. These celebs had far worse jobs before they were famous:

Brad Pitt: Danced around in a chicken suit for a fast food restaurant.

Rod Stewart: Worked as a gravedigger.

Johnny Depp: Sold pens by phone.

Christopher Walken: Was a lion tamer at a circus.

Tim Allen: Was a prisoner. He served two years for selling cocaine. (Now that's a shitty job.)

51. You live in a trailer park in Malibu.

Where do you live? It's one of the most common questions to ask people when you meet them. You proudly say Malibu and watch their reaction. Wow, Malibu. The first-rate beaches, homes, and breast implants. You've really made it, Mr. Tinstletown. Well, kind of. You do live in Malibu, but not in a million-dollar home. Not in a real home at all. Truth is you live in a trailer park within the Malibu city limits. Yes, even Malibu has trailer parks, and that's where your ass ended up.

The WTF Approach to Living in Your F*#!-ing Car

> **OPTION #1**

Keep quiet. You never have to tell anyone where exactly your "home" is located in the pretentious city. So whenever someone asks where in Malibu just say something like "Sorry I never give out my address" Or "Fuck off you crazy stalker."

> **OPTION #2**

Lie. If someone finds out you live in a trailer park, just tell them you just lost everything in the stock market and you couldn't bear to live anywhere but Malibu.

➤ OPTION #3

Make it trendy. Hey, who would have thought ten years ago that food trucks would be so popular. Make trailers parks the new food trucks. Start marketing trailer park homes to an upscale clientele and soon trailer parks will take over all of Malibu. Then it will just be another white trash town in America, yay!

➤ OPTION #4

Do nothing. So what if you live in a trailer park, at least it's not in Bakersfield. It's freaking *Malibu*! Who really gives a shit what you live in? Home is where the heart it, unless you really hate being poor. Then, get that trailer off the blocks and start looking for a city to park your house in.

➤ OPTION #5

Pimp your home. You've seen the show *Pimp my Ride*, well you need to pimp your home. "Trick" that shit out. Paint it purple and add a hot tub, make it awesome. Having the best trailer in the trailer park might not be so bad.

TRAILER PARK ALUMS

Eminem, Hillary Swank, and Kid Rock also lived in trailer parks, and look how they turned out. They're still white trash, but now they have money, so who gives a shit.

WTFACT: J. K. Rowling was living out of her car when she started writing the Harry Potter books, so park your trailer next to a school and playground and get inspired. No, not that way pervert!

WTFACT: Average beachfront home in Malibu is between $7 million and $17 million. Mobile homes in Malibu cost $2 million. Now that's some expensive white trash.

BEST PLACES TO LIVE

- Mansion
- Mansion on the beach
- Mansion on the beach with two blonde eighteen-year-old bisexual twin sisters who have daddy issues.

WORST PLACES TO LIVE

- An alley
- Your car
- Cleveland

52. You live in Los Angeles and you have asthma.

Tupac wrote a lot of songs about L.A., and if the city of angels is good enough for Pac, it's good enough for you. Endless sunshine, beautiful people, In-and-Out Burger—L.A. rocks. But there is one thing about L.A. that isn't so lovely— the smog. A cloud of soot hovers over the city like a fat man at a buffet table. This is bad enough for most, but with your asthma condition, going outside for you is a dangerous proposition.

The WTF Approach to Breathing in This F*#!-ing City

➤ OPTION #1

Go to the beach. L.A. isn't smoggy on the water where rich white people get to live. Become rich and white (if you aren't already) and move to sunny Santa Monica where the cool Pacific breeze blows away the smog.

➤ OPTION #2

Wear an oxygen mask. Not only is it a fashion statement, it's a political one as well. You'll be the trendiest dude in L.A. Before long you'll see Kim Kardashian rockin' an oxygen mask on TMZ, although wearing an oxygen mask might be inconvenient for her. Imagine having to remove it every time you wanted to perform oral sex on a basketball player.

➤ OPTION #3

Run for mayor and outlaw cars. Everyone who has been to L.A. knows that second to the smog (and resulting from it) traffic in L.A. is unbearable. Pass a law outlawing cars and build a transportation system befitting a modern metropolis.

➤ OPTION #4

Get a lung transplant. Obviously you were born with shitty lungs. Maybe if you get a new pair, maybe ones that come from Los Angeles, you won't have asthma. You will, however, take medications for the rest of your life and probably have to declare bankruptcy from the overwhelming doctor bills. But at least you won't be wheezing while you lose all your savings.

WTFACT: The grade of the air quality is the same grading system as school. A being the best, F is failing. Here's how your favorite city rates.

Montgomery, AL: D
Los Angeles, CA: F
Honolulu HI: A
Baltimore, MD: F
Camden, NJ: F
Jackson, OR: B

Wow. This country has some shitty air.

WTF: UP CLOSE AND PERSONAL

When my mother moved us to California from New Jersey, my Grandmother, a native New Yorker, asked her why. Mom said that she "loved it" there. Nana replied: "Fires, earthquakes, mudslides, and riots . . . what's not to love?"

—GB

53. You meet a girl in San Francisco—only to find out that it ain't no girl.

The Tenderloin is a neighborhood in San Francisco so-named for its beginnings as San Francisco's meat district. Porterhouses, rib eyes, NY strips, baseball steaks—in Old San Francisco the Tenderloin had it all. But today the Tenderloin offers a different kind of beef cut. Tranny cock anyone?

Yes, today the Tenderloin is a mecca for transsexual prostitutes. Really, really good-looking ones who can easily fool an unsuspecting traveler like yourself. So after meeting what you think is the girl of your dreams you discovered one fundamental problem with your otherwise perfect San Francisco Treat: It has a giant penis.

The WTF Approach to Dealing with a F*#!-ing San Fran Tran

➤ OPTION #1

Call Fox News. Sure you don't want to be famous for being the guy who took home a girl who had a dick, but Fox News pundits like Bill O'Reilly have a hard-on for San Francisco—and not in a good way. They'd love to have yet another anecdote to prove San Francisco's moral corruption.

> **OPTION #2**

Scream. Go ahead, let it out. Shriek like a girl. Who's going to judge you, the "girl" you picked up? Chances are he screams like a girl, too.

> **OPTION #3**

Commit suicide. San Francisco is a great city to kill yourself. You can jump off the Bay Bridge or the Golden Gate Bridge or take a skateboard down one of its many dangerously steep hills. However, if you prefer a more instantaneous death, go to Haight Ashbury and befriend some leftover Hippies from the 1967 Summer of Love. Get in the middle of a few of them in a tight space, exhale all the way, and breathe in the stench of forty-five-year-old patchouli oil. You'll be dead in no time.

DUDE LOOKS LIKE A LADY . . .

Celebrities who were caught with a tranny:

- Eddie Murphy
- Lil Bow Wow
- Lil Wayne
- Lamar Odom (Kloe Kardashian's husband)

AMERICA AIN'T NO JOKE

"It's not the first hooker that I've helped out. . . . I've seen hookers on corners and I'll pull over and they'll go, 'Oh, you're Eddie Murphy, Oh my God!' and I'll empty my wallet out to help," Murphy told *Entertainment Tonight*. "I'm just being a nice guy."

—Eddie Murphy after he picked up the tranny hooker.

54. You're homophobic and you get caught in the gay pride parade in San Francisco.

You like to think that you are not a bigot. You pride yourself on being open-minded when it comes to an individual's sexual preference. What two (or three) people do in the privacy of their own home is no one's business. That's the libertarian in you. But when you go to San Francisco to visit a friend, you take a wrong turn on the Cable Car and wind up in San Francisco's world famous Annual Gay and Lesbian Parade. All of a sudden you're surrounded by gays. And not just gays, but really, really gay gays. Suddenly you're panic-stricken. What to do when it's raining men and you don't even have an umbrella, let alone a way out of the crowd. You're stuck right in the middle of a throng of thongs. Yikes!

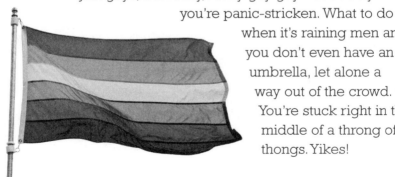

The WTF Approach to Being a F*#!-ing Homophobe on Gay Pride Day

➤ OPTION #1

Join the party. The only thing that gay guys like more than other gay guys are straight guys. If you look straight, they'll be on you like white on rice. Strip down to your underwear and throw a boa around your neck. Fit in and they'll leave you alone. Then sneak out the back door before they sneak *in* your back door.

➤ OPTION #2

Call Fox News. The conservative Fox News pundits aren't the biggest fans of the Gay Pride Parade. Call them up and have them send in a helicopter to rescue one of their homophobic comrades in danger.

➤ OPTION #3

Point and shout "Cher!" Scream and point that you have sighted Cher in the Parade. While everyone goes nuts and starts running in that direction to pay homage to the Queen of Queens, run like hell.

➤ OPTION #4

Realize you are gay. Just like the conservative evangelical preachers who are always caught schtupping a teenage boy, realize that you are so homophobic because deep down, you are looking for some consensual man love. Then enjoy yourself as the new proud gay man you always wanted to be but were afraid to admit.

the rainy states above california

55. You get transferred to Seattle and you've never been so depressed.

Every place has it upsides and its downsides. For instance, New York City is the most exciting city in America. That's the upside. The downside? It's expensive and smells like piss. Los Angeles has perfect weather. That's the upside. The downside? Well, just about everything else. Seattle is a beautiful city, surrounded by gorgeous snow-capped mountains and lush green forests. The downside? The constant rain makes you want to kill yourself.

The WTF Approach to Dealing with Overwhelming Depression

> **OPTION #1**

Go to a coffee shop. According to studies, caffeine can help counteract depression. The home of Starbucks and The Coffee Bean & Tea Leaf, Seattle is known as a coffee shop town. Go hang out, pretend to read Proust, and lis-

ten to some grungy high school dropout do a poor cover of a Pearl Jam song. Jesus, that's even more depressing.

> **OPTION #2**

Read *This Boy's Life*. The touching coming-of-age story from master memoirist Tobias Wolfe follows the teenage boy's troubles growing up in the Seattle area. Compared to his shitty life with his evil stepfather, your life in Seattle will look blessed by comparison.

➤ **OPTION #3**

Watch *Frasier*. The great Seattle-based sitcom about psychiatrists Dr. Frasier Crane and his brother Niles might give you some insight into your psychological state. If not, it'll be good for a few laughs.

➤ **OPTION #4**

Get light therapy. Seasonal Affective Disorder (SAD) is a recognized condition. The main treatment for this is bright light therapy, which consists of sitting by a special broad-spectrum lamp from thirty minutes to three hours a day. If this and/or pills don't cheer you up move on to option #5.

➤ **OPTION #5**

Jump off the Space Needle. Seattle is no stranger to suicides, so make your exit from this world a little more dramatic and get the attention in death that you always craved but never received in life.

TOP FIVE SUICIDAL DESTINATIONS

1. Port Moresby, New Guinea—also called the city of AIDS—every year it infects 115,000 more.
2. Linfen, China—a city with no sunlight because of overwhelming dust in the air.
3. Burundi—the poorest country in the world
4. Chernobyl—irreversibly destroyed by nuclear catastrophe
5. Your childhood bedroom—nothing good ever happened in there

56. You live in Oregon and you're not a logger or a lesbian.

Oregon is one of the most physically beautiful states. The rocky coastline and glimmering green meadows are simply breathtaking. Interestingly, the beauty of this land is starkly contrasted by the ugly, smelly people who inhabit it. (Just kidding. They're probably not that smelly). But seriously, Eugene, Oregon, is not Miami Beach. Most Oregonians are either loggers or hippie environmentalist lesbians. Oddly, they share little in common except a mutual love of flannel. But you're not a logger and you have no interest getting into the hippie lesbian business. Or maybe it's the other way around? Either way you just can't seem to fit in. Every time you head to a micro-brewery, you feel left out. WTF?

The WTF Approach to F*#!-ing Fitting in with the Oregonians

➤ OPTION #1

Man up. Be a logger. Or dress like one. Flannel shirts, mullets, and unkempt beards are back in style now. Today you can't tell the difference between a logger and a hipster. So man up and get rugged. Who knows, you might even go home with a couple lesbians? Sure they aren't the hot lipstick lesbians. Not exactly Mila Kunis and Natalie Portman in *Black Swan*, but it's something. After all, you're in Oregon.

➤ OPTION #2

Head East on the Oregon Trail. Get the hell out of there and head the opposite way the pioneers did. Unfortunately the trail will end at Independence, Missouri. Chances are people there look like shit too.

➤ OPTION #3

Start a makeover show. Get on public access TV and host a show that turns loggers into ladies men, and hippie lesbians into, well, Mila Kunis look-a-likes.

➤ OPTION #4

Try Portland. Oregon may be mostly loggers and butch lesbos, but Portland has one of the highest per capita strip clubs in the nation. True you'll see mostly loggers and butch lesbians stripping, but they'll be the best looking loggers and lesbos in Oregon, the pride of the state.

57. You get kidnapped by a band of hippies along the Oregon Trail and are held for ransom at a Phish concert.

You've always loved American history, particularly the history of the West. You can't wait to set out along the Oregon Trail, retracing the great pilgrimage once braved by pioneers longing for a better life. Zipping along in your new motorcycle, you can almost see the line of covered wagons stretching into the distance. Your excursion takes you through Kansas, Nebraska, Wyoming, Idaho. Finally you see the sign, "Welcome to Oregon." You've made it. What an experience! Just when you look up at the great big Western sky and thank God for this trip you hear the ominous sound of a Volkswagen bus. Indians? No, these guys are much more hairy—and more dangerous. OMG! Hippies! Ah! You accelerate and leave them in the dust. But there are more. Ahead you see a road block of several VW buses. Uh-oh. A hippie ambush. Fast forward several minutes of futile resistance and you're tied up in the back of a VW bus headed for a Phish concert. WTF?

The WTF Approach to Being F*#!-ing Kidnapped by Hippie Hooligans

➤ OPTION #1

Pay. Give these hippies what they want—money for drugs and to fight environmental injustice. Clear out your bank account and save your hide. Any more of this Phish music and you'll go insane!

➤ OPTION #2

Pray. This time it will work. God hates hippies. All that peace and love, nonsense. He likes real men who work for amoral corporations and advocate an ill-conceived all-out invasion of Iran.

➤ **OPTION #3**

Convert to Hippie-ism. If you decide to convert, they might not kill your yuppie ass. Okay, so you'll miss bathing regularly and you don't like dressing like a Native American. And you prefer your women to sport a Brazilian wax, not a bush of pubes thicker than the surrounding forest. And let's not even go into the torture of a drum circle. But remember the good things about hippies. They're peaceful. Well, not the ones that kidnapped you, but most of them. And the girls are loose and like to party. And, other than Phish and the Grateful Dead, hippie music rocks. Plus, you can throw all that career stress away. Being a loser here is a *good* thing. So put on some tie-dye and chill, man.

WTF: UP CLOSE AND PERSONAL

I once went to a Phish concert because there were drugs and girls who I thought would have sex with me. I was right on both counts. I had heard a little Phish, but not enough to where I had any opinion. Turns out that they are the worst, most annoying band in the history of music. And the people! My God, the people! They are so bizarre and ridiculous, it's actually much more of a trip to not take acid and go sober.

—GB

chapter eight

the south shall not rise again

58. You lose a banjo duel to a creepy kid with no eyes and you pay the price.

One day on vacation you and your fellow city slickers head down to the backwoods of Georgia for a little taste of nature. You, a proud banjo player, can't want to play with some real hillbilly players out in the woods. You find your match. A creepy kids who looks blind. He agrees with a smile to challenge you, but instead of money he'll play for your soul. Thinking this kid has seen one too many movies, you agree. Please. How good can this little brat really be? Holy shit, he's amazing. You play until your fingers bleed but to no avail, this kid clearly kicks your ass. When it's over, you try to shake his hand only to realize this is no ordinary kid. "See you in hell," he says. WTF? Did you just lose your soul for real?

The WTF Approach to Losing Your F*#!-ing Soul to a Kid

➤ OPTION #1

Start praying. Get your ass to a church, a temple, a mosque, or wherever you go and beg God to take your soul back. How could you have known this kid worked for the devil? Then go on the road giving sermons about devil children who are musically inclined. If you can't save yourself, save someone else.

➤ OPTION #2

Squeal like a pig. Face it, you're screwed—right in your asshole. A deal is a deal and you must pay up. Get your affairs in order and get ready for hell. Oh, but before you go, live it up doing everything you're not supposed to do; you're already going to hell, so who gives a shit.

➤ OPTION #3

Kill the kid. A deal is a deal, but only if the deal maker is alive, right? Find the kid and take him out. You might feel bad because he's a kid, but remember he's also the Devil's bitch. Send his ass straight back to hell and get on with your life.

➤ OPTION #4

Up the ante. Find this soul sucker and make another deal with him. Make him an offer for something better than your lousy soul, like the soul of someone who is really a good person, like your wife. Maybe he'll accept the deal; maybe he won't. But you'll never know without trying. Then you can keep your soul and enjoy being single again.

IN THE FUTURE . . .

Never challenge a blind kid at anything. What are you a monster?

59. Country roads don't take you home—but to a Starbucks.

It has been a long time since you've been back to your West Virginia hometown—or even spoken to anyone there. Driving down the winding roads, you are flooded with memories of your childhood here, the sweet sounds of John Denver in your ear. You think of Grandpappy drinking moonshine and telling stories on the porch, Ma in the kitchen cooking up another road kill surprise. And Pa coming home in a drunken rage looking for someone—anyone—to beat the living shit out of. Ah yes, those were the days.

It's good to be back. So far everything looks the same. Old Johnson's farm still smells like a combination of sweat and feces, and Willy the three-legged dog with seven kinds of cancer still hobbles along the road. But when you get to your street there's one big difference—one momentous change. Where the fuck is your house?

You check the street names and confirm that you are in the right place. Yep, this is the corner of Loser Lane and Black Lung Blvd. But where your house used to be there is a store. You get close and put on your brights. Is that a fucking Starbucks? WTF?

The WTF Approach When All Roads Lead to F*#!-ing Starbucks

➤ OPTION #1

Burn it down. Sure, it's arson, but you'll be doing the neighborhood some good. Also, even if you are convicted, you can probably run into a lot of your family members in jail. Maybe that's where they all went when the house was demolished.

➤ OPTION #2

Have a latte. Or a double espresso. You need to wake up and investigate the disappearance of your house with a clear, sharp mind.

➤ OPTION #3

Open up a Coffee Bean. Wherever there is a Starbucks, a Coffee Bean is around the corner. Set up shop and drive that Starbucks out of business.

➤ OPTION #4

Head back to civilization. Listen, you left that dump of a town long ago for a reason. Don't try and romanticize it. It was dirty, muggy, and everyone looked like shit.

WTFACT: There are approximately 11,168 Starbucks in the United States in all fifty states. One of the only places they don't serve Starbucks is in prison, so feel free to drive your car into that Starbucks.

STARBUCKS IS NO LAUGHING MATTER

● Starbucks says they are going to start putting religious quotes on cups. The very first one will say, "Jesus! This cup is expensive!"—Conan O'Brien

60. You re-enact the Civil War and you make the South win.

Every weekend it's the same thing. You get your friends together, put on your uniforms, grab your rifles and head out. Not to shoot up a mall, you re-enact what you consider to be one of the greatest wars in history, the Civil War. Sure, there are many groups of people who gather to play out how the South was defeated, but in your re-enactment the South wins. The only problem is that your "fans" (the loser tourists who gather to watch you) get really mad—and those muskets you're carrying don't shoot real bullets. WTF to do when faced with a nerdy mob?

The WTF Approach to Rewriting F*#!-ing History

➤ OPTION #1

Stand your ground. Literally, keep doing what you're doing; maybe you'll end up confusing the tourists who come to see you and people will start to believe the South really did win. And while you're at it, bring back slavery.

➤ OPTION #2

Get over it. Seriously, how long can you do this? We don't just mean pretending the South was victorious. We mean how long can grown men get dressed up in ridiculous uniforms and play out a war that's long been over?

Start acting like a real man and go to a sports bar and get wasted like other guys. Then you can be proud of things the south does have, like racists and *Toddlers and Tiaras*.

➤ OPTION #3

Go on the road. Take this act on the road and show people what it would have been like if the South *did* win. Maybe it will catch on and other groups will re-enact other wars like World War II. Make the Germans win. That should draw a crowd.

HISTORICAL EVENTS AND TIME PERIODS THAT SHOULD *NOT* BE RE-ENACTED

- The Spanish Inquisition
- The Black Plague
- The Dust Bowl
- The Holocaust
- The Disco Era

for the ladies . . .

Please. No real woman would waste her time doing this.

61. You were born and raised in Mississippi and you still need the song to spell it.

It happens every time you have to enter your address. Mrs. M, Mrs. I, Mrs. Double S I, Mrs. Double S I, Mrs. Double P I. Got it. Despite living in this state your entire life you can't seem to remember the spelling without singing that stupid song we learned in grade school. Don't even think about moving to Massachusetts.

The WTF Approach to Graduating from Third-Grade Spelling Level

> **OPTION #1**

Move to Iowa. Just four little letters, so easy. Of course, now you have another issue: what the fuck is there to do in Iowa besides same-sex marriage.

> **OPTION #2**

Get tested. If you lived in Mississippi your whole life and you still can't spell it on your own, then you obviously have some issues upstairs.

> **OPTION #3**

Get a tattoo. Get Mississippi tattooed on your arm; that way you will never forget how to spell it. All you have to do is look down. Careful, though. Make sure your tattoo guy spells it correctly, or else you'll be screwed.

OTHER WORDS THAT PEOPLE TEND TO MISSPELL.

- Cincinnati
- Obviously
- Conscience
- Daiquiri
- License
- Misspelled

WELCOME TO
MISSISSIPPI
Birthplace of America's Music

62. You live in Alabama and your name is Kevin Kale Kerry (K.K.K.).

When your parents picked your name, it wasn't some malicious attempt to ensure a childhood of misery for their son. They just wanted to honor their family. They picked Kevin, after your grandfather on your father's side, and they picked Kale after your grandfather on your mother's side. They figured one day you would feel honored to be named after two great men. But, as you have long known, your parents are morons. Kevin Kale Kerry? K.K.K.? WTF?

The WTF Approach to Living with a F*#!-ing Racist Monogram

➤ OPTION #1

Reject your name—and your family. Find a new family. You really want to be a part of a family that is either so stupid or so racist or both that they name you K.K.K.?

➤ OPTION #2

Leave town. Hey, why should you have to change your name just because your initials happen to be identical to one of the most violent terrorist organizations in American history? Move to where

there are no African-Americans
that will take offense. Try Maine.

> **OPTION #3**

Hide. Hurry! Your name is KKK for
Christ's sake! Run!

for the ladies . . .

As long as you're hot it doesn't matter
what your initials are. Hotness trumps
racism!

63. Your granddaddy was the grand wizard of the KKK.

Your family has never really talked about your grandfather. And when someone mentioned him, everyone seemed to shift uncomfortably in their seats. You never really cared that much about it until you found out why. Turns out your granddaddy was famous. Not famous for acting or writing or composing music. No, your granddaddy was famous for something else: lynching black people. You're granddaddy was the grand wizard of the Ku Klux Klan. WTF!?

The WTF Approach to Dealing with the Sins of Your Racist Grandfather

> **OPTION #1**

Play the adoption card. Tell people that you were adopted. When the rest of your family hears this they will probably be very upset, but who cares, they should have thought of that before having children.

> **OPTION #2**

Flip the switch. Sure, your grandpappy was racist and horrible, but everyone has skeletons in their closets. Find out some dirt about your friends' relatives and throw it back in their faces.

Match the child to their horrible famous father.

1. Benito Albino   A. Osama bin Laden

2. Salem   B. Kim Jong-Il

3. Han-sol   C. Mussolini

Answers: 1. C; 2. A; 3. B

64. You're the only Middle Eastern family in Arkansas.

Your parents decided to come to America to give you a better life. They wanted only the best for you. But unfortunately, they weren't very smart people. When deciding where to live they picked Arkansas. Good choice, morons. Enter a young Arab kid in junior high school in white-bread Arkansas. Exit an Arab junior high school kid with a chip on his shoulder the size of a commercial airplane that, with the right training, could be grossly misused.

The WTF Approach to F*#!-ing Living as a Muslim in Arkansas

➤ OPTION #1

Open a mosque. If you build it they will come. The other Muslims, that is. Send out an SOS to the Middle Eastern community that Arkansas is the new Middle East.

➤ OPTION #2

Embrace it. It's better to stand out than blend in, right? Find those girls who really want to piss off their daddies and start banging them.

Make your penis larger. Look, if all those girls are gonna come running to have sex with you, better have something to impress them with. Also, if some red neck wants to start a fight with you one night, just show him your huge dick; he will either shut his mouth or shoot you. Either way, problem is solved.

WTFACT: California has the largest Middle Eastern immigrant population in the United States, with nearly 40,0000.

65. You're on a diet . . . in Mississippi!

Welcome to Mississippi! The fattest state in the country in the fattest country on Earth! And Mississippi has held on to this title for six straight years! A diet for native Mississippians consists of sacrificing an extra order of bacon with their fried chicken, waffles, grits, and biscuits and gravy.

But regardless, they love food like they love Elvis—a fucking lot. But you're on a diet. How to live in a world fried, glazed, and dipped in fat?

The WTF Approach to Being on a F*#!-ing Diet in Mississippi

➤ OPTION #1

Starve yourself. Not only will you lose weight, you might show poor people in Mississippi what being poor is supposed to look like—the way it looks in every other part of the world. (We aren't being pricks here; poor people in the United States are fatter because they eat bad foods, whereas poor people in other countries don't have access to any food— let alone bad food. If you think you'd kill for a bag of Doritos after a blunt, imagine what an Ethiopian kid would do?) Wow, that was sad and weird. For funny, go to Option #2.

> OPTION #2

Go Atkins. The good thing about being in a place where people eat like animals is that there are a lot of animals to eat—and animals are low carb, and high protein, the fundamental principle of the unbelievably unhealthy but nevertheless effective Atkins Diet. In the Deep South you'll find chicken cooked in butter, catfish cooked in butter, and shrimp cooked in butter. If you're not into butter, you can dip any of the above dishes in cheese, lots of cheese, and still follow your Atkins regimen. Your heart might explode, but you'll lose weight for sure.

> OPTION #3

Date a fatty. Hey, it's all relative, right? Date a fat girl there and you'll feel better by comparison. True, she is not as hot because she is fat, but you'll look better by comparison.

> OPTION #4

If you can't beat 'em, join 'em. Hey, the South is a fun place. People live life there. They party, they eat, they drink—they live life to the fullest. Even if that life is cut short due to obesity. So get rid of your bullshit elitist coastal attitude and join the party. Don't worry; no one is going to see you when you become your bigger, jollier self. After all, who the fuck is going to ever come visit you in Mississippi?

ORGANIC FOOD CRAZE

Everyone—except in Mississippi apparently—is hopping on the organic food bandwagon. Cage-free, pesticide-free, preservatives-free; everything is "free" this and "free" that. One question: If all this natural food has nothing extra added to it, why the fuck does it cost more money? It should cost less, no? Not to mention most of these organic treats taste like a steaming gluten-free pile of dog shit.

And then there are the raw-food people. What the fuck is their story? Humans have been cooking their food for hundreds of thousands of years.

Fucking *Homo erectus* knew how to grill hamburgers. Now all of a sudden it's bad for us? Bullshit.

WE'RE NUMBER TWO!

Coming in at a close second as the home for the fattest fucks in America is the great state of Alabama. Who knows, they might just steal that number one title away. Watch your backs Mississippi—and your backsides.

Rounding out the top ten are:

3. West Virginia
4. Tennessee
5. Louisiana
6. Kentucky
7. Oklahoma
8. South Carolina
9. Arkansas
10. Michigan

So, the top five fattest states are in the South. Why? Because they fry *everything*. Studies show that Southerners believe that second only to the Cotton Gin the Deep Fryer is the best invention of all time.

TOP FIVE FRIED THINGS IN THE SOUTH

1. Chicken
2. Potatoes
3. Twinkies
4. Snickers
5. Crosses

WTFACT: Alabama has its own Obesity Task Force. We imagine it goes something like, "Sir, please step outside the vehicle and out of the drive-thru lane. Now walk fifty paces, stop to catch your breath, and eat a fucking salad."

66. You piss off a voodoo priestess in Louisiana.

You came to Louisiana looking for fun. Good food, great jazz, and of course, Mardi Gras. You decide to go to some of the local voodoo shops, not because you believe in that shit, but just because it's kitschy and could be fun. While there, you meet a real voodoo priestess—who turns out to be a lot hotter than you expected. Full of a few too many hurricanes, you start flirting. She warns you to stop, but you're buzzed and having a good time. Then this freaky bitch starts muttering in a strange language, and spits on your shoe. WTF? Turns out you just pissed off a voodoo priestess and she's about to put a hex on your ass. Oh shit.

The WTF Approach to Dealing with One Very Pissed off Voodoo Bitch

➤ OPTION #1

Do nothing. The saying goes that if you don't believe in voodoo, then nothing can happen to you. So forget about that silly crap and get on with your life. And if you happen to get a horrible disease or get hit by a truck, you'll know that saying was bullshit, whoops.

➤ OPTION #2

Make amends. Who cares if you did nothing wrong? Bring her flowers or a chicken to sacrifice—something to get on her good side. Do whatever it takes, then get the hell out of Louisiana and keep your mouth shut from now on.

➤ OPTION #3

Flip the switch. Two can play at that game bitch. Hire your own voodoo priestess and start a voodoo war.

WTFACT: According to *Urban Dictionary*, voodoo also refers to vodka mixed with Mountain Dew.

IN THE FUTURE . . .

Stick to asking women to show their tits on Bourbon street for plastic beads.

WTFACT: Voodoo priests and priestesses are also known as witch doctors.

67. You run out of moonshine on a Friday night in rural West Virginia.

When someone says "West Virginia" you usually think of two things: incest and that John Denver song about driving on country roads. But a close third would have to be moonshine, homemade liquor deep in the Appalachian mountains. Ever since you can remember, every night there was always moonshine to be had.

Until you ran out, shit!

The WTF Approach to Scoring Some More F*#!-ing Shine

➤ OPTION #1

Beg, borrow, and steal. You live in West Virginia for God's sake; you probably can't throw a rock without hitting another person making moonshine. Go and ask to borrow some. If they say no, beg for some. If they still say no, steal that shit. Bring a gun, of course; those fuckers are crazy.

➤ OPTION #2

Switch it up. Your drink that is. Go to the store and get some good old-fashioned whiskey. It will probably taste like water to you, but after a couple of bottles you should start feeling the effect.

➤ OPTION #3

Make more. The whole point of drinking that shit is because it's homemade. Just go make more you drunken hillbilly. Then find one of your cousins and start making out. That's what the shine will make you do!

WHAT'S IN THE SHINE?
The basic ingredients for moonshine are corn meal, sugar, water, yeast, and malt.

MOONSHINE IS NO LAUGHING MATTER

"You can tell it's good if you light it and a blue flame comes up; that means it's good moonshine and it won't make you go blind."

—Johnny Knoxville

68. Your wife keeps showing her breasts for beads and it isn't even Mardi Gras.

Let's face it. You didn't marry her for her brains. You married her for those deliciously round flesh bags hanging gently from her chest. She's got a pair, all right. So it wasn't a shocker that she likes to show them off, especially during that infamously fun-filled week in New Orleans, good ol' Mardi Gras.

There's only one problem: Mardi Gras ended a week ago. Yet still she insists on pulling up her shirt, flashing everyone on the street and yelling for beads. She does it in restaurants. She does it in coffee shops. She even flashed the congregation at church. She just won't stop. No matter how many times people tell her Mardi Gras is over, she refuses to accept the party has died. The woman has gone insane—and needs to be stopped.

The WTF Approach to Controlling Your F*#!-ing Flashing Wife

➤ OPTION #1

Buy her a chastity bra. Like a chastity belt, a chastity bra is an iron-clad brassiere incapable of being taken off without the key. You didn't decide to put up with her idiocy so everyone else could see her tits. These are just as much your tits as they are hers. Now only you, the key holder, will have access to these beautiful boobs.

➤ OPTION #2

Flip the switch. Start taking off your top in public and ask for beads. With the weight you've been putting on recently, your tits are probably bigger than hers. In fact, step it up a notch and start flashing your testicles to everyone you see. Two can play at that game.

➤ OPTION #3

Have her institutionalized. Take the necessary action to have her put away for treatment. When she shows the judge her tits and asks for beads it should be a no-brainer.

➤ OPTION #4

Give her a complex. Sometimes, even the most attractive, sexy woman is just one insult away from insecurity. Tell her that her tits are beginning to sag. That'll be the end of that.

➤ OPTION #5

Divorce her. You really want to be married to a flasher? Make sure to at least get visitation rights to her tits in the divorce settlement.

➤ OPTION #6

Make her famous. Send the pictures of her tits to *Playboy* or another nudie magazine and make some cash. If she's gonna show the world her boobs you might as well reap the rewards. That way you'll have some cash to pay for therapy.

WTFACT: The first Mardi Gras parade was in the 1830s, but the beads tradition didn't start until sometime in the 1920s. Makes sense; everyone knows women in the 1830s had ugly tits.

IN THE FUTURE . . .

Don't marry a slut!

WTFACT: When someone wants beads they are supposed to yell "Throw me something, Mister!" Coincidently, that's what prostitutes also yell. Each color signifies a different meaning:

Purple—justice
Green—faith
Gold—power
Any color—show me your tits! Now!

69. You're the only person in your Tennessee town who believes in evolution.

Americans are a special people. We developed nuclear weapons, landed on the moon, developed the iPhone. Science and innovation is what has driven this nation's economy since the cotton gin. But at the same time we are the only modern Western nation debating whether or not we should teach creationism alongside evolution. In your small hometown in Tennessee, everyone you know is a creationist. No one believes in evolution. "Hell, if you want to think you came from monkeys that's your own darn business, but I didn't come from no monkey." And so goes the ridiculous arguments you are sick to death of. Despite the unpopularity of your position you just can't accept this religious nonsense. But you love your town. WTF?

The WTF Approach to Being a F*#!-ing Darwinian in Small Town Tennessee

➤ OPTION #1

Convert everyone. Most of the time, people who reject evolution don't actually understand the scientific theory. Go door to door and try to break down difficult concepts like natural selection. Hey, if a Jehovah's Witness can convince a stranger to give up celebrating their birthday, you can convince these folks to accept the theory of evolution.

➤ OPTION #2

Fake it to make it. Just go along with everyone and accept the fairy tales they embrace. Statistics show that religious people are happier and live longer than cynical, soulless pricks like you. Sure they're obviously delusional, but at least they don't think about suicide at night like you do.

➤ OPTION #3

Go to a Goth Club. Even in Tennessee there are goth clubs in the big cities. Take a drive and find like-minded people who believe that God is dead like you.

GOTH CLUBS IN TENNESSEE, ACCORDING TO THE INTERNATIONAL GOTH CLUB LISTING

- Temple, Knoxville, TN
- MIG Project, Memphis, TN
- Salvation, Nashville, TN
- Subversion, Nashville, TN

WTF IS UP WITH CREATIONISM AS A "SCIENCE"?

Please. A scientific theory must be proven; it requires evidence. What is the evidence proving creationism is true? A collection of Jewish short stories and the occasional citing of the Virgin Mary in a grill cheese sandwich? Oh, that's right, there is evidence of a flood. Okay, well even if that is true, it doesn't mean that the explanations given in the biblical account are true. Just because the actual city of Troy made famous in Homer's epic was discovered in the nineteenth century, thus proving that the battle of Troy as immortalized in *The Illiad* really did occur, are we also to believe that Athena came down every half hour to check it out? Same logic here. Just because there was a flood doesn't mean that a 700-year-old Jewish guy named Noah got all the animals on the boat and told them to fuck.

WTF MULTIPLE CHOICE QUIZ

Which of the following groups accept creationism as described in Genesis?

A. Jewish people
B. Muslims
C. Christians
D. Mormons
E. All of the above

Answer: E

70. You're a teetotaler on a diet living in New Orleans.

New Orleans is the undisputed home of great food, great drinks, great jazz, and the occasional hurricane that destroys an entire city and makes getting wasted while eating great food at a jazz club more difficult. It was the food and the booze that seduced you to move to the Big Easy from your stale Northeastern town, but after two years of po' boys and hurricanes (the drinks, not the tropical storm) you've gone from a lean and mean muscle machine to a fat, drunken pig. Now you're off the booze and off the crawfish. WTF are you going to do in this town now?

The WTF Approach to Being a Party Pooper in the Big Easy

➤ OPTION #1

Have sex. Sure, sex is not nearly as good when you aren't full of gumbo and alcohol, but it's still something you can find easily in New Orleans. You don't need to drink bourbon to get laid on Bourbon Street—so long as you find a chick who has drunk enough bourbon for two.

➤ OPTION #2

Take pills. Prescription pills are a growing problem in this country. They're a lot of fun and they have no calories. Develop an Oxy-Contin habit and you'll be just as wasted as everyone else—without the carbs.

➤ OPTION #3

Move somewhere crunchy. Get out of New Orleans and go spend time with other lame-ass party poopers like yourself. Take up yoga in your new home and eat vegan food. You'll probably end up living another five to ten years. Sure, it will be a fucking boring five or ten years, but it's something.

➤ OPTION #4

Move to England. Those Brits love a good cup of tea. Oh wait, they also love to drink. Screw it.

FAMOUS TEETOTALERS

- Natalie Portman
- Frank Zappa
- Mahatma Gandhi (duh!)
- Alice Cooper
- Adolf Hitler

YOU MIGHT BE AN ALCOHOLIC IF . . .

When you pee, the toilet reeks of beer

You went home with what you thought was a woman, but woke up with a man

Instead of 75 percent water, your body is 85 percent whiskey

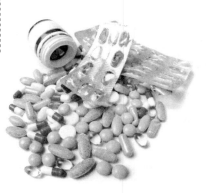

71. Everyone in church handles snakes, but you're too scared.

>>>> *And these signs shall follow them that believe; In my name shall they cast out devils; they shall speak with new tongues; They shall take up serpents; and if they drink any deadly thing, it shall not hurt them; they shall lay hands on the sick, and they shall recover.*

—Mark 16:17–18

While most of us don't take this biblical passage as Gospel (wink wink), you do. But the thought of holding a venomous snake scares the living shit out of you—and everyone in church knows it.

The WTF Approach to Being a F*#!-ing Snake Handler

➤ OPTION #1

Convert. Convert to something sensible, like Judaism. There will be no chance you will ever be surrounded by snakes. Candles, yes. Snakes, no.

➤ OPTION #2

Take the plunge. Come on, what's the worst thing that can happen? Oh, the snakes are poisonous? Oh, well, yeah. That's some serious shit.

➤ OPTION #3

Get one of those mechanical toy snakes. Let's face it, people in your church aren't the sharpest pencils in the box. Try a mechanical toy snake and see if you can fool them. Chances are they grew up so poor they don't even know what a toy looks like.

WTFACT: For the movie *Snakes on a Plane* over 450 snakes were used. The movie *Raiders of the Lost Ark* used over 1,000 snakes. That basically means there are more working snakes in Hollywood than actors.

SNAKES ARE NO LAUGHING MATTER

"Always carry a flagon of whiskey in case of snakebite, and furthermore always carry a small snake."
—W. C. Fields

"I have no fear of losing my life—if I have to save a koala or a crocodile or a kangaroo or a snake, mate, I will save it."
—Steve Irwin

"Never wound a snake; kill it."
—Harriet Tubman

WTF ABOUT TOWN

- WTF: So you are going to hold a venomous snake to show your faith in God.
- Lunatic: I reckon I am.
- WTF: Hmm. I reckon you're a goddamned idiot.
- Lunatic: Hey buddy, don't take the Lord's name in vain.
- WTF: See what I mean?

72. Your pappy and your grand-pappy were coal miners—but you love musical theater.

My Fair Lady. The Sound of Music. Oklahoma. Ah, there is nothing like the sights and sounds of a Broadway musical. Ever since you were a boy you've wanted to leave your rural Appalachian town and head to the Big Apple to make it in musical theater. But your family has a long tradition in the coal mining business. Your pappy and your grandpappy were both coal miners, and they'll be dammed if you are going to go off and be some sissy-boy singer in the big city. Wouldn't you rather spend hours upon hours each day covered in soot at the bottom of a cave and then later die of black lung? What the hell is wrong with you, kid?

The WTF Approach to Living Out Your F*#!-ing Dreams

➤ OPTION #1

Wait until they die. Grandpappy should go anytime, now. As for pappy, he's too drunk to know what the hell is going on. Wait until he passes out on some moonshine and leave town.

➤ OPTION #2

Write a musical about coal mining. Maybe pappy and grandpappy will be more supportive of your musical theater aspirations if you paid homage to the proud coal mining tradition in your family.

➤ OPTION #3

Tell them that Jesus Christ, your personal savior, told you not to be a coal miner but to pursue your Broadway dreams instead. Do they really want to deny Jesus the opportunity to see you perform a solo in *Miss Saigon?*

➤ OPTION #4

Give up your dreams. You're never going to make it anyway. Give up your dreams just like everyone else in your town does. Then take to drink, and beat the shit out of anyone you see.

➤ OPTION #5

Build a theater in the mine. Think about it; you'll have the first underground theater in history. The acoustics should be pretty good down there. Work during the day, perform at night. And if there is an accident and the mine caves in, you'll give new meaning to "bringing down the house." Sure, everyone will probably die, but at least they saw a good show first.

POSSIBLE TITLES FOR YOUR COAL MINING MUSICAL

- West Side Coal Story
- How to Succeed in the Coal Mining Business Without Really Trying
- A Funny Thing Happened on the Way to the Coal Mine
- Fiddler in the Coal Mine
- The Best Little Coal Mine in Texas
- The Coal Miner's Son
- Guys, Dolls, and Coal Miners
- The Coal King

73. You get attacked by really attractive vampires in rural Louisiana.

There are vampires, and then there are the vampires of rural Louisiana—think HBO's *True Blood*. These cold-blooded hotties are always looking for a little midnight snack. One balmy summer evening you're taking a late-night stroll when all of a sudden three of the most attractive vampires you have ever seen jump out of the trees and stand right before you. You don't know whether to run or to cum. Wait . . . what?

The WTF Approach to Surviving an Attack by F*#!-ing Vampires

➤ OPTION #1

Run. You won't get very far. These aren't zombies, moron. Vampires are fast. Lightning fast. That's why they screw so well.

➤ OPTION #2

Cum. Go ahead; you know the sight of hot vampire girls and guys standing before you about to eat your flesh off the bone and leave you dead in a puddle of your own blood gets you excited. Why wouldn't it?

➤ OPTION #3

Break out the *True Blood*. You should always carry a six pack of *True Blood* on you when walking through rural Louisiana. Duh!

➤ OPTION #4

If you can't beat 'em, join 'em. Get bitten and become a vampire. Just think, you'll be crazy strong and you'll live forever. And remember, there is always self-tanning spray.

WTF IS UP WITH CHICKS DIGGING VAMPIRES?

True Blood is porn for women. And forget about *Twilight*—a movie that is single-handedly responsible for the rise in teenage pregnancy. Not to mention the rate of vampirism. What do women find attractive about a pale, cold dead guy biting them until they turn red with blood? Just don't get it. Now, the steamy werewolf thing makes sense. Weres run hot, after all. Heck, who doesn't want to fuck Jacob? Wait . . . what?

> **WTFACT:** Eighty percent of preteen girls got their first period while watching *Twilight: New Moon.*

HOW WELL DO YOU KNOW YOUR VAMPIRES?

Match the vampire to the movie or TV show.

1. Bill Compton
2. Edward Cullen
3. Angel
4. Dracula
5. Maximillian
6. Selene
7. Lestat

A. *Buffy The Vampire Slayer*
B. *Interview with a Vampire*
C. *Underworld*
D. *Twilight*
E. *True Blood*
F. *Dracula*
G. *Vampire in Brooklyn*

Answers: 1. E; 2. D; 3. A; 4. F; 5. G; 6. C; 7. B

the great white north

74. You live in Fargo, North Dakota, and you haven't seen the movie.

There aren't that many towns in America made famous by a film, but the film *Fargo* really put Fargo, North Dakota, on the map. It was an Academy Award–winning film that brought people across the country to see if it was just like in the movie. With the cold and those crazy accents, "don'tcha know"? You have lived in Fargo now for some time, and whenever you tell someone that, you get the same thing: "Oh, like the movie!" Problem is, you've never seen the movie. You just like living there. If you hear about this movie one more time you might just lose your shit. Damn those Coen brothers!

The WTF Approach to Not Being in the Know, Don'tcha Know

➤ OPTION #1

Lie. When people start talking about the movie, just pretend that you've seen it. If someone refers to a specific part in the movie just say, "Wow it's been so long since I've seen it, I just don't remember," then quickly change the subject.

➤ OPTION #2

See it already! For God's sake it's only about two hours long; just sit down one night and watch the damn movie. It won a few Oscars so it can't be all that bad, and if it helps there is a scene with a man and a wood chipper, enjoy!

➤ OPTION #3

Flip the switch. Start talking about another movie based in Fargo and give people shit about not seeing it. Truth is, there probably isn't one, but they don't need to know that. "What?! You've never seen *Best Little Whorehouse in Fargo*?

What do you live under, a rock?!" On second thought, you should make that movie.

➤ OPTION #4

Kill the Coen brothers. They made the damn movie that's ruining your life. Go find them and kill them. Then make a movie about that!

FARGO QUOTES: JUST A FEW REASONS TO SEE THIS MOVIE

- "Ya got Arby's all over me."
- "Shep! What the hell are you doing! I was bangin' that girl!"
- "Oh my. Where? Yeah? Aw geez. Okay, there in a jif. Real good, then."

WTFACT: The Coen brothers claim the movie *Fargo* is based on true events that happened in Minnesota in 1987, the opening even says "Based on true events." That was a lie. The Coen brothers knew more people would go see it if they thought it had really happened. See? Lying can be good, and profitable.

75. You can't seem to shake that ridiculous Minnesota accent.

Sure, when you lived in Minnesota it was fine; everyone sounded like you. But now you live in Seattle, and thanks to your ridiculous accent, no one knows what the fuck you're saying. You feel like a foreigner in your own country. You get looks and eye rolls from people. You thought accents were hot. Well, some accents. British, French, even a New York accent can get a woman excited. But a Minnesota accent? That's just fucking lame.

The WTF Approach to Losing That F*#!-ing Midwest Speech Impediment

➤ **OPTION #1**

Hire a vocal coach. It's just an accent, for God's sake. If you work on it long enough you should be able to get to a point where people barely hear it anymore. Sure, it might take time and a little money, but with that vocal handicap you're never gonna get laid again. Think of it as an investment for your dick.

➤ **OPTION #2**

Do nothing. Screw those people if they can't understand you. You know what you're saying. Go on and be proud of that horrible, grating accent! You betcha!

➤ OPTION #3

Flip the switch. Pretend that it's everyone else who has a crazy accent. Say "Huh? What? Come again?" Let those fuckers see how annoying and frustrating it is. After a while no one will want to talk to you, but who cares; conversation is so overrated.

➤ OPTION #4

Make your penis bigger. If you make your dick larger, then it doesn't matter if anyone understands you. A huge penis is universal. Guys will respect you and women will want to reproduce with you, stupid accent and all. So the next time someone makes fun of that accent, whip out your dick. That will shut them up.

IN THE FUTURE . . .

Don't leave Minnesota, idiot.

WTF TRANSLATION

Here are some real phrases one might hear while in Minnesota and their meanings.

"Ohh, Dae-vuht, how'ss werk going fer yuh thesse dayss?"

Translation: "Hello David, how is it going at work?"

"Pleassse feed the shickens fer me, will yuh?"

Translation: "Please feed the chickens."

"Yah sure, you betcha, Uff-dah, Lutefisk with some pins, don't'cha know?"

Translation: "Don't have sex with a tranny without a condom, what are you, a fucking moron?"

BEST ACCENTS TO HAVE
- British
- Australian
- South African
- French

WORST ACCENTS TO HAVE
- Boston
- Canadian
- German

76. You're the only black person in your Montana town.

You have always loved living in Montana. The air is clean, the land is vast, and the people are . . . white. Really white. In fact you soon realize that not only are you the only black person in your town, but you are the only nonwhite person period. You stick out like a sore thumb, a black sore thumb. How to fit in when you clearly stick out?

The WTF Approach to Filling the Ethnic Quota

➤ OPTION #1

Repopulate. Start banging chicks and reproducing. It's about time they got some color up in that town. Sure, the babies will only be half black, but half is better than nothing.

➤ OPTION #2

Move your family up there. If you can't wait till your babies grow up, then move your family to this town and take that shit over. Soon you'll be the majority. Take that, crackers!

➤ OPTION #3

If you can't beat them, join them. Deny your heritage and pretend to be white. When someone points out the fact that you're a black person act surprised, "What?! I am??" And just to prove them wrong, be really bad at dancing.

WTFACT: Portland, Oregon, is the whitest city in America.

for the ladies . . .

Don't let these white assholes bring you down. The guys are mean to you because they know their dicks are too small, and the girls are jealous because your ass can't double as a frying pan.

77. You meet the love of your life while hiking the Appalachian Trail.

It's always been a goal of yours to hike the Appalachian Trail. You have trained and planned for this, and now you're on your way. Nothing is gonna stop you. Wait a second. Who is that hottie? No, stay focused—you still have a long way to go. But seriously, she is amazing. You would love to check out her "Appalachian Trail." You start to follow her, hoping you can strike up a conversation next time she stops to take a rest and then right before you can say a word, she heads off in a different direction. You never believed in love at first sight, but you have to find this woman . . . . Problem is, you still have 500 miles to go.

The WTF Approach to Finding True Love on a F*#!-ing Hike

➤ OPTION #1

Invite her along. Introduce yourself and invite her along on this amazing journey you are taking. If she declines then at least get her name and number so when you finish this insane hike you can find her again.

➤ OPTION #2

If option #1 doesn't work, grab her hot ass off the trail and force her to continue on with you.

➤ OPTION #3

Forget her. You said you were gonna finish this hike and you have to keep your word; it doesn't matter how hot this chick is. If it's meant to be, it will happen, or so all those stupid self-help books promise. Let her go; if she comes back to you it was meant to be. And if she doesn't, find another girl who looks like her and marry her instead.

➤ OPTION #4

Stop hiking. Why the fuck are you even making this crazy hike? So you can say you did it? Just lie to everyone and say you completed it. Photoshop yourself in all the landmarks and call it a day. Then you can stay in the town where this amazing woman is from and get to know her. When you tell people you're getting married they won't even give a shit about that ridiculous hike you were on, they'll just be happy that you finally found someone to marry your lame ass.

HIKING IS NO LAUGHING MATTER

"Hiking is like sex. You think you can do a lot, until you get into it."
—Anonymous

BIGGEST DANGERS ON THE APPALACHIAN TRAIL

- Weather conditions
- Human error
- Plants
- Animals

WTFACT: Hikers that attempt to complete the entire trail in a season are called Thru-hikers. As in "Are we fucking thru this shit yet!?"

WTFACT: Traditionally, only about 10 percent to 15 percent of those who make the attempt report to the Appalachian Trail. We are assuming the other 90–85 percent stop during the hike because they come to their senses.

WTFACT: The trail passes through the states of Georgia, North Carolina, Tennessee, Virginia, West Virginia, Maryland, Pennsylvania, New Jersey, New York, Connecticut, Massachusetts, Vermont, New Hampshire, and Maine. Damn that's a lot of work!

vegas, baby!

WTF?

78. You wake up in Vegas with a new wife.

"What happens in Vegas, stays in Vegas." We all know the expression—and for the most part it's true. The adult playground does have a reputation for bringing out the naughty side in us all—and then lets us sweep it under the carpet and return to our normal, ever-so-dull everyday lives. But when you wake up after a night of drinking and partying only to find a wedding ring on your finger—and a strange girl lying next to you—you realize that leaving this in Vegas ain't going to be that simple. You're married! Married! WTF?!

The WTF Approach to Waking up in F*#!-ing Vegas Married

➤ STEP #1

Stay calm. Remember the yoga class your real wife made you take with her and take a deep breath. If you really need to shake the hangover and get your head straight and calm your nerves,

make yourself a Bloody Mary. But just one! After all, that's how you got here in the first place.

➤ STEP #2

Go to the ATM. Take out some cash—if you have any left after your night of partying—and spend the $147 you need to in order to file a Complaint for Annulment with the Clark County Court.

➤ STEP #3

Wake wifey up. Naturally you want her to keep sleeping (forever if possible), but you are going to have to wake her up and convince her that last night was a mistake and that you need to get the marriage annulled. It will be much more difficult to get annulled if she's not on board.

➤ STEP #4

Tell her you are dying. If for some reason she doesn't want to untie the knot, confess to her that you are dying of some rare illness and have only three months to live. And that you want to spend your last days with your mother, not a stripper from Déjà Vu.

➤ STEP #5

Tell her you are her brother from another mother. According to the State of Nevada there are several grounds for annulment, including if the two spouses are related by blood. Tell her that you first sought her out just to reconnect with your lost sibling, but that the connection was so strong you ended up sleeping with her. If she buys this, chances are she'll be on board with the annulment—the minute she stops throwing up.

WTFACT: Nevada leads the United States in number of divorces per capita.

GROUNDS FOR ANNULMENT

- Lack of consent of a parent or guardian
- Lack of understanding/insanity
- Fraud
- Spouses that are closely related by blood ("Closely?" Gross!)
- Either the plaintiff or defendant was married to someone else on the day the plaintiff and defendant were married

WORSE THINGS TO WAKE UP TO THAN A WIFE

- An STD
- One less kidney
- A man named Bubba standing over you

CELEBS WHO GOT MARRIED IN THE LITTLE WHITE WEDDING CHAPEL

- Sinead O'Connor
- Sylvester Stallone
- Freddie Prinze Jr. and Sarah Michelle Gellar
- Britney Spears
- Rita Hayworth
- Shane Barbi and Ken Wahl
- Patty Duke, first and third husbands
- Mary Tyler Moore
- Paul Newman and Joanne Woodward
- Judy Garland
- Joan Collins
- Slash, first wedding
- Steve Austin
- Bruce Willis and Demi Moore

79. You go to the Bunny Ranch expecting to see rabbits.

What could seem more wholesome than a bunny ranch? A ranch populated with little fluffy white rabbits with cute little ears and bushy tails is what you expected when you overheard those guys in the casino going on and on about what an amazing time they had at the Bunny Ranch.

"Remember that one with the tail?" the fat one said.

"For sure," the other man said. She was something all right. I had to stop myself from tossing her in a cage and taking her home with me."

But it turns out that you—and your very pleasantly surprised thirteen-year-old son—weren't going to see any rabbits that day. Beaver? Yes. Bunnies? Not so much.

The WTF Approach to Accidently Walking into a F*#!-ing Whore House

➤ STEP #1

Cover your son's eyes. Don't let him see the scantily clad women walking around in lingerie, their tits pushed up to their chin. Sure, he's thirteen, but he's never seen women with little or no clothes on. How do you know? Well, because he's ugly, that's how.

➤ STEP #2

Tell your son to wait in the car. You're going to have to forcibly remove him from the scene, throw him in the passenger seat, and tell him if he gets out you'll kill him. Save him from this unwholesome and ungodly scene.

➤ STEP #3

Give them a piece of your mind. How dare they let women walk around like that practically half-naked, their supple, delicious cleavage hanging over their corsets, a garter hugging each smooth, milky thigh. Bastards! Perverts! Animals!

➤ STEP #4

Give them a piece of your penis, instead. Not permanently, as some sort of sick memento, just for a half hour or so. The Devil always wins.

➤ STEP #5

Feel guilty. That's right, after the moment of orgasm go back to your car feeling a little bit poorer both in dollars and in spirit.

➤ STEP #6

Come back a week later and do it all over again.

WTF RANT

Why do they only have brothels for men? As a single gal I can tell you I would love to go to a place where I could pick from a lineup of hot men to fulfill my every need. I would also love to have a menu of services to choose from at the Dick Ranch.—JM

What's great about the Bunny Ranch is the services they provide. Check out the actual menu from The Bunny Ranch:

- Girlfriend experience
- Massage (give or get)
- Hand relief party
- Vibrator show
- Bachelor parties
- Orgies
- Dungeon
- Blow job
- VIP rooms
- Champagne party
- Pamper party
- Love at the Y
- Half and half
- Bunny style
- Viagra party
- 69 party
- Full French
- Around the world
- Tantric sex
- Asian wet room
- Swinger parties
- Sybian experience
- Dinner dates
- Neapolitan

- Whipped cream party
- To-go orders
- Military discount
- Two-girls party
- Overnight stays
- Outdoor & indoor Jacuzzi fun
- Fetish & fantasy
- Couples and single ladies
- Three-girls party
- Food, fun (9½ weeks)
- The porn star experience

for the ladies . . .

Menu at the Dick Ranch

Fix my sink
Fix my car
Fix my toilet
Fix my water heater
Fix my self-esteem

80. What happens in Vegas does not stay in Vegas.

You tried to be good. You really, really did. But she was sooo hot. And you were sooo drunk. And your girlfriend was sooo far away. Plus, it's Sin City, right? You are supposed to let loose and get crazy. At least your girlfriend back in Cleveland will never know about it. Ha, that's what you think. When you come home all your stuff is out on the lawn. Turns out you weren't the only one in Vegas getting wild, your girl's coworker was there too. And guess what, you fucked her. WTF?

The WTF Approach to Getting F*#!-ing Caught Cheating

➤ OPTION #1

Deny. Deny. Deny. Just keep denying no matter how mounting the evidence is. Maybe she has the wrong Michael. Even if her coworker points you out right in front of your girlfriend and says you are the dude she screwed just keep denying. Even if she knows intimate details about your scrotum, still deny. If you never admit it, you always have a chance.

➤ OPTION #2

Say you were drugged. Tell your girlfriend you were drugged and you were going to tell her but you didn't want to worry her. Tell her that you must have been slipped a rufie and then was date raped by this crazy woman. Obviously she has it out for you and is willing to do anything to destroy you. To destroy *us*.

➤ OPTION #3

Bring flowers. Being some flowers and say you are sorry and that you won't do it again, and that you love her and that you will go to counseling and that you are a changed man and that you will never, ever take her for granted again and that you only have eyes for her. Then feel guilty for knowing deep down in your heart you'd bang another woman in a minute if you could get away with it.

➤ OPTION #4

Flip the switch. Guilt her by saying that you do not feel loved or appreciated and that she never tells you how beautiful you are anymore. Girls are used to guys acting like little bitches these days, she might end up apologizing and consoling *you.*

WTF ABOUT TOWN

Girlfriend of Cheater: Hi.

Coworker: Hi.

Girlfriend of Cheater: I heard you went to Vegas last weekend. I'm so jealous. How was it?

Coworker: Awesome.

Girlfriend of Cheater: My boyfriend Michael just went there.

Coworker: (smiling) That's funny. I met this really hot guy there named Michael. He lives here in Cleveland, too. I'm really excited.

Girlfriend: What does he look like? I mean, I'm just curious; of course, it isn't the same Michael (she laughs nervously).

Coworker: He looks like your boyfriend. Because he is your boyfriend.

Girlfriend of Cheater: What!?

Coworker: Ha, ha. I fucked him *real* good. Oh, did I mention I am being promoted to director? The announcement is being made today. Well, I have to get back to work destroying lives. Ta Ta for now!

Girlfriend of Cheater: I am going to eat Häagen Daaz and watch *The Holiday* until I drown in a puddle of my own tears.

for the ladies . . .

Don't worry; guys are oblivious. They wouldn't notice if you came back covered in semen, let alone if you had an indiscretion in Vegas one night. Of course, guys are jealous and will treat you like you are a cheater even if you're innocent, so you might as well get some action.

81. You bet your house and savings on craps and lose!

You've always considered yourself a responsible gambler. But tonight you are in the zone; it seems you can't lose. Every game you play you win. And then you see it, that beautiful seductive craps table just calling your name. You start playing, and things are going well, but then something happens, and the tide turns. Now you're losing big time. Your brain is telling you to cut your losses and walk away, but your stupid gut is trying to convince you that you can win this back. Just need one big win. So you bet everything, all your savings. Your kids' college savings, the mortgage to your house, and there go the dice. Rolling, rolling, rolling . . . SNAKE EYES. Oh well, looks like the only thing staying in Vegas is your money. No wonder they call it craps.

The WTF Approach to Losing It All in F*#!-ing Vegas

➤ OPTION #1

Fake your own death. Hopefully you took out some life insurance when your kids were born. Your policy should cover your losses. If you don't have a life insurance policy, well at least everyone will think you are dead and you won't have to deal with the aftermath.

➤ OPTION #2

Regroup. It's Vegas for God's sake, you can win this back! Or at least pay off some of the debt. If you really have nothing left to cash in, start selling yourself. There have to be plenty of rich gay dudes or ugly chicks that would pay for play. Start fucking, buddy.

➤ OPTION #3

Become a gypsy. Go get your kids and hit the road. Go from town to town and sleep where you can.

Find some other gypsies and join their colony or whatever those freaks call it. Make beads and shit and sell them on the beach. It might feel nice to live off the land, so to speak.

➤ OPTION #4

Do nothing. Hey, there's probably a part of you deep down that thought to yourself, "If I wasn't tied down with this mortgage and kids, I could be a rock star." Well, now you can. Stay in Vegas and start a rock band. The kids will get over it. Well probably not, but who cares? They're not your problem anymore. Rock on.

IN THE FUTURE . . .

Stick to nickel slots, you're not ready for the big time.

VEGAS IS NO LAUGHING MATTER

- "The only game I ever seem to win in Vegas is the ATM."—JM

- "Last night I stayed up late playing poker with Tarot cards. I got a full house and four people died."—Steven Wright

- "I like to play blackjack. I'm not addicted to gambling, I'm addicted to sitting in a semi-circle."—Mitch Hedberg

- "If you're playing a poker game and you look around the table and can't tell who the sucker is, it's you."—Paul Newman

82. You find out your daughter is a stripper in Vegas.

When your only daughter told you she was moving to Las Vegas to be a performer, you encouraged her. She has a good singing voice and has always been outgoing. Then a week after she gets there she calls to tell you she got hired to perform in a show. Wow! You're so proud of her. You offer to fly out and see her perform, but she quickly shuts you down. "I'll be too nervous if you're there, Daddy." Oh how sweet. So you tell her you understand but secretly book a flight to see her. She won't be nervous if she doesn't know you're there, right? You ask the cabbie to take you to The Femme Fatale show. He smiles and nods. Oh, he must have seen the show, you think. When he pulls up to your stop, you immediately realize this is no show where your daughter shows off her vocal prowess—this is a strip club. Maybe this is the wrong place, but since you're there, maybe you'll go in for just one drink. The first dancer, Lola, comes out. She looks a little familiar. . . . Oh fuck. Lola is your daughter. Your little girl is a stripper in Vegas.

The WTF Approach to Having a Daughter Taking Her Clothes Off for a Living

➤ OPTION #1

Sneak out. Get out of there quick before she sees you. Then head over to the first bar you can find and get wasted. You can deal with the problem tomorrow. Tonight you just need to blackout.

➤ OPTION #2

Spank her. You're her father and she's been very naughty. Wait. Never mind.

➤ OPTION #3

Start yelling. Stand up and scream, "Stop staring at my daughter's tits!" She will be horrified, the customers will be confused, and the bouncers will quickly throw your ass out.

➤ OPTION #4

Kill yourself. Truth is if you were a better parent she wouldn't be a stripper. It's all your fault this happened, so end your life and save yourself the grief and embarrassment of people knowing what your daughter does for a living.

➤ OPTION #5

Support her. Sure this isn't what any father wants for his little girl, but if she's gonna strip the best place for her to be is in Vegas. She could make a lot of cash there. It's her life, so show her that you support her. In fact go out and buy some flowers to give to her when her little dance is over.

for the ladies . . .

If your daughter is a stripper then you should start stripping with her. People will pay big bucks for a mother/daughter act.

IN THE FUTURE . . .

Have a fat ugly daughter.

WTF RANT

Why are strip clubs called "gentleman's clubs"? When is the last time you went to a strip club and saw a gentleman there? Gentlemen open doors for women and pull out chairs. The "gentlemen" at these clubs only pull out their dicks, and their wallets.

HOW MUCH CAN A STRIPPER MAKE IN VEGAS? IT ALL DEPENDS ON THE VARIABLES . . .	
Looks and Hygiene	**Wages**
Ugly + Clean	$
Ugly + Dirty	$$
Hot + clean	$$$
Hot + dirty	$$$$

83. You wake up hungover in Vegas and can't find your buddy.

You loved the movie *The Hangover* so much that you and your friends decided to head to Vegas and have your own adventure. You drank, gambled, went to strip clubs, drank some more, and then passed out. You wake up the next morning with a pounding headache, a black eye, and a burning sensation when you pee. Pretty standard stuff, so far. But one thing is not to be expected. Your friend is no where to be found. He's vanished. You try to retrace your steps from the night before but after the fourth Jager shot things got fuzzy. WTF, your life really is *The Hangover*.

The WTF Approach to Finding a Missing Friend in F*#!-ing Vegas

> ### OPTION #1

Do nothing. Look, you were able to get your drunken ass back to the hotel room last night, so it's not your problem if your friend got lost. He'll probably turn up soon, and if not, charge the room to his card.

> ### OPTION #2

Call the cops. Don't try to solve this like they did in the movie; this is real life and you need the professionals for this one. Let the cops look for your friend between doughnut breaks while you continue to party.

➤ OPTION #3

Leave now! Something really bad probably happened, and you need to save yourself. Pack your shit and get the hell out of there. What happens in Vegas stays in Vegas, and it looks like your friend is what happened.

➤ OPTION #4

Put up posters. Just like when someone loses their cat or dog. Download a picture of your friend and slap that shit all over the city. You might not find him, but you will probably find some little hottie who feels bad for you. Girls always like to help guys look for shit. You might get lucky in a different way. Maybe if she's clean it will cancel out last night's tryst and that burning sensation will go away. Oh, it doesn't work like that?

for the ladies . . .

Do nothing; it was probably her fault anyway.

IN THE FUTURE . . .

Go to Reno, it's much smaller.

WTFACT: According to the *Las Vegas Review Journal* about 1,000 people go missing in Las Vegas each month.

chapter eleven

rocky mountain high

84. You live in Aspen and the high altitude keeps making you sick.

Y ou've always been fascinated with the Rocky Mountains and the beauty of Colorado. You know a few people that moved to the Centennial State from the big city and never looked back. Finally you give up your day job and land a gig at a hotel in Aspen. Your new life has begun. On the way up the mountains, you revel at the physical beauty of the Rockies, inhaling the clean mountain air. Slowly, however, you start to slow down. Your breathing gets shorter, faster. You feel dizzy. You're nauseous; you can hardly breathe. Are you dying? Well, maybe. You've got altitude sickness, and it's all downhill from here.

The WTF Approach to Surviving High F*#!-ing Altitude

➤ OPTION #1

Build up your tolerance, just like when you started drinking. You couldn't always drink a case of beer and be fine. You had to start slow. Start at a lower elevation and build your way up. Soon you'll be able to reach the top of a mountain while drinking a case of beer. Now *that's* talent.

> **OPTION #2**

Smoke up. It's a fact that marijuana helps with nausea and headaches, which are some of the symtoms of altitude sickness, so go out and get that long overdue medical marijuana card and light up. Now you'll really know what it means to be Rocky Mountain high.

> **OPTION #3**

Get an oxygen tank. You're feeling sick because you're not getting enough oxygen, so strap one of those little portable tanks to your chest and get moving. Just be careful when you light up a cigarette or you'll have another problem on your hands.

WTFACT: Altitude sickness or mountain sickness is very similar to being hungover —except you might die. So skip the mountain hike and just get wasted. It's safer and a lot less strenuous.

TOP FIVE MOST HORRIBLE THINGS THAT EVER HAPPENED IN THE MOUNTIANS

1. The Donner party. Not a "party" at all, really. In the winter of 1846, hundreds of pioneers heading to California from Missouri got stuck in the snows of the Sierra Nevada mountains. About one-half starved to death. The others resorted to cannibalism to survive. Party on!
2. The other gross cannibal story about those plane crash survivors in the Andes in the movie *Alive*.
3. Any one of the several dumbass hikers who get eaten by a mountain lion each year.

4. Every time that lazy-ass Smokey the Bear prevents a forest fire. Or, more accurately, convinces others to prevent forest fires while he gets all the glory. Because only YOU can prevent forest fires! Right, Smokey? Well then, one has to ask, *What the fuck do we pay you for then, Smokey?*

5. When Jude Law dies at the end of *Cold Mountain*. Soooooo sad!

for the ladies . . .

Mountains? Um, I'll be in the lobby of the hotel getting my nails done. Thanks!

TOP FIVE GREATEST THINGS TO HAPPEN IN THE MOUNTAINS

1. Gay love affair in *Brokeback Mountain*. Not good for the wives of the men, really. But for them, totally! Well, except in the end, anyway.

2. The time WTF? Author Bergman received oral sex when he was twelve by a college girl at camp. Who da' man now, bitches?

3. The time WTF? author Jodi Miller gave a kid oral sex at camp. Wait! Greg, was that you?

4. When Hannibal crossed the Alps with hundreds of elephants in order to attack Rome. That is fuckin' gansta!

5. The last time Greg Bergman went snowboarding on the weekend and he landed that killer jump! Hell yeah, dude! That was so extreme, bro!

85. Turns out there is nothing to do in Denver when you're dead.

You love Denver, always have, and now always will. You just had a massive heart attack while shoving down hot wings at Hooters, and you're dead, in Denver. Luckily, you seem to remember a list of things to do in Denver when you're dead. But so far, the afterlife is really boring.

The WTF Approach to Enjoying Your F*#!-ing Afterlife

> **OPTION #1**

Start haunting people. Shit, it's your afterlife; do what you want. Pick someone you've always hated and make his life miserable. Then find all the women you have wanted to see naked and start haunting them.

> **OPTION #2**

Look for a light. It's time to move on, so find that big, warm all-consuming light and go into it

already. Unless you don't see a light, then you're probably going to hell. If so, then stay in Denver and go back to option #1.

> **OPTION #3**

Find a medium. There are plenty of people who claim they can communicate with the dead. Find one of those and start up a friendship. Ask her what to do when you're dead.

THEY SEE DEAD PEOPLE: SOME VERY FAMOUS MEDIUMS, IN REAL LIFE OR ON SCREEN

- Sylvia Browne
- James Van Praagh
- George Anderson
- Patricia Arquette

WTF: UP CLOSE AND PERSONAL

Famous medium John Edward says that all our loved ones watch over us constantly, which freaks me out. Not because I don't believe in ghosts but because if that is true that means my very Jewish grandmother watches me masturbate drunk while crying.

—JM

86. You inherit an Aspen Chalet but are terrified of skiing.

Aspen is known for many things. The restaurants, the scenery, the skiing. It's where the rich and famous go to get away and relax. So when you found out you inherited a chalet from a family member you should have been excited. Instead, you're terrified. Not only can you not ski, but you also hate fucking snow. WTF?

The WTF Approach to Dealing with Your F*#!-ing Snow Phobia

➤ **OPTION #1**

Exposure therapy. Immerse yourself in the snow and get over your fear of skiing. Sure you will probably get frost bite and lose some toes, but at least you won't be scared of skiing anymore.

➤ **OPTION #2**

Take lessons. You're in Aspen, asshole; take some lessons and learn how to ski. Or maybe snowboard. Find a hot ski instructor to show you how to do the snowplow technique, then snowplow her.

➤ **OPTION #3**

Fake it. Buy the ski clothes and pretend to be an expert skier. Hang out at the local bars in your ski gear and talk about how great the slopes were. No one's going to question you.

➤ OPTION #4

Fake an injury. Put one of those removable casts on your leg. When someone asks what happened, tell them you broke your leg doing a flip on the slopes. You'll probably get some ass this way too. Women love a guy who is injured.

➤ OPTION #5

Become a drunk. Start drinking a lot. Then people will know you as that guy who owns that chalet and drinks too much. No one will let you near the slopes.

➤ OPTION #6

Sell it. This is a no brainer. A chalet in Aspen has to be worth a lot; sell it and move to Hawaii, unless you're also scared of surfing, then you're screwed.

SKIING IS DANGEROUS: FAMOUS PEOPLE WHO DIED DUE TO ACCIDENTS ON THE SLOPES

- Sonny Bono
- Natasha Richardson
- Michael Kennedy
- Mitch Hedberg (okay that wasn't on the slopes, but it was a different kind of snow—cocaine)

87. You get attacked by a bear while camping.

You've always loved camping. Pitching a tent, cooking your food over a fire, and sleeping under the stars. Ah, the great outdoors. Know who else loves camping? Bears. Well actually they love campers. You've heard stories about the people who get attacked by bears, but you never thought it would happen to you. And then . . . Wait what's that sound? Aw, it's a bear. Look how cute he looks, like one of those cartoon bears from the toilet paper commercials. Then he gets closer. Oh shit. That's a big fucking bear!

The WTF Approach to Surviving a F*#!-ing Bear Attack

➤ OPTION #1

Play dead. It's a fact that in a bear attack you're supposed to just lie there and play dead, the bear will quickly get bored and leave, unless you really are dead, then problem solved.

➤ OPTION #2

Bargain with the bear. Throw some of your food at the bear and see if he bites. If that doesn't work offer up your friend as food instead of you. Sure, your friend will hate you, but on the bright side he will probably be dead soon.

➤ OPTION #3

Fight back. Don't be a little pussy and let this bear kill you. If you're gonna die, then go out fighting. Grab a rock or stick and attack back. You might not live to tell about it, but at least you'll have a good story to tell in Heaven. Hopefully there is not a bear in heaven to fuck your ass up when you get there.

➤ OPTION #4

Start singing. It always works in those Disney movies. Why not try it? Unless you're a really bad singer, then the bear might just maul you because you're pitchy.

There are different tactics when encountered with different bears. Check out how to deal with:

GRIZZLY BEARS

- Lie in fetal position and cover your head
- Play dead

BLACK BEARS

- Use bear pepper spray
- Don't climb a tree
- Fight back

POLAR BEARS

- Offer him a job as the spokesperson for Coca-Cola

IN THE FUTURE . . .

Bring a gun to fend off bears or other campers who want to go all Deliverance on your ass.

for the ladies . . .

Why the fuck are you camping anyway?

88. You accidently start a forest fire.

Smoking is a bad habit. It's smelly, expensive, and ultimately it kills you. But that's your business, no one else's. But when you toss a lit cigarette in a dry patch of grass and cause a massive forest fire, that is someone else's business. Holy shit! The entire mountain is on fire! You should have paid more attention to Smokey Bear when he said "Only you can prevent forest fires." Smokey is gonna be pissed!

The WTF Approach to Surviving a F*#!-ing Forest Fire You Started

➤ OPTION #1

Fight fire with fire. See if the old adage holds any water. There should be plenty of fire there already. Harness some and fight the rest of the fire with it. See what happens.

➤ OPTION #2

Get serious. Call the forest rangers and let them know that there is a fire burning out of control. They'll take it from there. When they ask you if you know how it started you might not want to be puffing on a Marlboro.

➤ OPTION #3

Get lost. Leave all your shit behind (remember to take the kids, though) and run away. Don't call to report the damage. Plenty of forest fires are caused by lightning. It's nature's way of renewing the forest. So fuck it. What's one more?

WTFACT: Four out of five forest fires are caused by people. The fifth is started by bears; they're such pranksters.

for the ladies . . .

This is a good thing, especially if you're single. Start a fire and sit back for the hot firemen to arrive.

IN THE FUTURE . . .

Don't smoke in the forest idiot!

WTF RANT

Why do we say fight fire with fire? What a stupid saying, and it doesn't make sense. Who is looking at a fire and thinking "Wow look at that fire burn, we need to fight it. No not with water with fire. Yes, we will fight that blazing inferno with more fire; that should put it out. Oh wait . . . that doesn't seem right. Oh well fuck it, it looks pretty." Come on people it's time for a new saying!

the two that got away (alaska and hawaii)

89. While in Alaska you get attacked by a moose.

You can't believe you are actually in Alaska. Home of Eskimos, The Klondike Bar, and brainless former governors. And it's also beautiful. You enjoy your time skiing, ice fishing, and having sex with Alaskan hookers. Then one day while out for a walk you see a moose. "I have to get a closer look," you say to yourself, awestruck by the animal's beauty. You've heard the warnings about getting too close to a moose, but fuck it; you need a great pic for Facebook. You move in, then suddenly out of the blue the moose starts charging. You're about to be impaled on moose antlers!

The WTF Approach to Getting Attacked by a F*#!-ing Moose and Living to Tell about It

➤ OPTION #1

Run! Come on, it's a moose not a mountain lion. Start running, asshole. If the moose starts gaining on you, climb up a nearby tree, then call out for help like the pussy you truly are.

➤ OPTION #2

Start recording. When have you ever seen anyone attacked by a moose? If you survive this attack you can upload it to YouTube and get millions of hits. You'll become famous as the moron who pissed off a moose and got trampled.

➤ **OPTION #3**

Scream. That's right, start screaming like a little girl. Hopefully someone will hear you and come out to help you fend off the moose. If they can't, then maybe the moose will start to attack them while you get away.

IN THE FUTURE . . .

Admire the moose from afar, moron.

90. You're from Eek, Alaska, WTF?

You're from Eek, Alaska, population: 281. Need we say more? It sucks balls, and you can't wait to get the fuck out of there, but you can't get out. Just not in the cards, right now. No money and no will. What to do?

The WTF Approach to Living in F*#!-ing Eek

➤ OPTION #1

Make it great. Turn Eek, Alaska, into a great vacation destination— get some funding and open restaurants and hotels; build some luxury condos. It's remote; it's beautiful; it could be the perfect retreat. If you work hard at it, you can make this the new Aspen. Except without all the beautiful people of course.

➤ OPTION #2

Destroy it. That's right, burn it to the ground. Then people will talk about it as a legend, Like Atlantis. Some will write stories about it and songs. Maybe people will come and try to resurrect this tiny town and make it great. You, of course, will probably be in prison, but at least there will be more people there than in Eek.

➤ OPTION #3

Do nothing. Who cares if you live in the middle of nowhere? Do you really want to be with the rest of civilization? Working around the clock to make something of yourself so you can show off to everyone? Fuck no. Stay in your small town and live out your life there without any ambition at all. You'll probably be happier.

➤ OPTION #4

Change the name. Maybe no one comes to Eek because it's named Eek. Petition to change the name to Awesomeville or Brad Pittsburg. Maybe that will make you feel better the next time you have to tell people where you're from. It's still in Alaska, though, so it won't help that much.

SIZE MATTERS

Lost Springs is the smallest town in the country. Located in Converse County, Wyoming, only 1 person lived there as of the 2001 census. Wow. He must really enjoy his own company.

OTHER SMALL TOWNS

- Deals Gap, North Carolina—pop. 6 people
- Rendville, Ohio—pop. 29 people
- Jacksonburg, Ohio—pop. 37 people

91. You're a recovered alcoholic living in Anchorage, Alaska.

>>>>> Y ou've done the steps, got the chips, and are proud to say you are three years sober. Good for you. It's been a hard road, but now you feel like you're finally over the hump—until you get transferred to Anchorage, Alaska. Shit, don't they like to drink a lot there?

The WTF Approach to Staying Sober in F*#!-ing Alaska

> **OPTION #1**

Find a meeting! Yes, those Alaskans love to drink, but that means there have to be other recovering alcoholics hiding out somewhere. Do a search and find an AA meeting. Get a new sponsor and work the program.

> **OPTION #2**

Start drinking. You live in Alaska now, so who gives a shit if you're a drunk? In fact, open a bar; that way you can make money while supporting your habit. Cheers!

> **OPTION #3**

Don't leave the house. You can only be tempted if there's something to tempt you. If you stay home and never leave you won't be tempted to hit the bottle. Tell your company you have to work from home for health issues. If they don't like that and fire you, then you can get the hell out of that cold drunken state and get back to the civilized world.

WTFACT: Alaska is known for it's problem with alcohol, but its claim to shame is that it has the highest per capita suicide rate in the nation. Then again, what would you do if you lived next to Sarah Palin?

for the ladies . . .

Who cares if you're an alcoholic? Men outnumber women six to one in Alaska, so drink up.

92. You move to Hawaii and you can't swim.

Hawaii. Land of violent volcanoes, calm sandy beaches, and tourists looking for swimming, sun, and sex—and not necessarily in that order. You were excited to relocate to Hawaii. It certainly beats Cleveland. But there is only one problem with your moving to this tropical beach paradise. You can't swim. WTF?

The WTF Approach to Not F*#!-ing Drowning

➤ **OPTION #1**

Learn. It's never too late. Sure you'll look like the world's biggest jackass pathetically flailing around in a pool with floaties on your arms like a two-year-old, but a man's gotta do what a man's gotta do.

➤ **OPTION #2**

Become really, really fat. Screw swimming, just get fat enough to

where you can just float and not worry about going under. Watch out for whale poachers though— you don't want to end up in some fish market in Tokyo.

➤ **OPTION #3**

Make the chicks come to you. Why do you have to get in the water anyway? Sit on the beach and call the ladies to you. What's that? You're scared of the sand? Well, then we really can't help you.

IN THE FUTURE . . .

Be born to parents who care enough to teach you how to swim.

WTFACT: Aquaphobia is known as the fear of drowning. An aquaphobe may get anxious even looking at a clear glass or pitcher of water. Really, a pitcher of water? Pussy. Anyway, common symptoms of aquaphobia include anxiety, dizziness, nausea, increased heart rate, and of course, the biggie: drowning.

WAYS TO DIE THAT ARE SCARIER THAN DROWNING

- Being burned alive
- Electrocution
- Being skinned alive
- Falling into a vat of sulfuric acid
- Flesh-eating bacteria
- Flesh-eating girlfriends
- Old age in New Jersey

93. You can't fall asleep in Anchorage because the sun won't go down.

Living in Alaska has many benefits. It's cheap, it's beautiful, and you can see Russia from your porch—making you an immediate foreign policy expert. But the downside of all that northern exposure is the especially long nights in the winter and the especially long days in the summer. You never expected it to be a problem, though. Nothing a few blackout curtains can't fix. But like Pacino in *Insomnia* you just can't seem to get any shuteye—and it's driving you mad.

The WTF Approach to Getting Some F*#!-ing Sleep

> ### ➤ OPTION #1

Take a pill. Not a sleeping pill, but a pill designed to make you less of a pussy and a more of a man that doesn't need sleep. A real cowboy never sleeps. So man up and deal with it.

> ### ➤ OPTION #2

Count sheep. Counting sheep is a great way to lull oneself to sleep. Luckily for you, you don't even have to use your imagination, since you live in the middle of fucking nowhere. Just look out your window and count the sheep and caribou and polar bears and other animals on your lawn.

➤ OPTION #3

Build a bomb shelter. If blackout curtains and dark sunglasses don't help, then crawl into a bomb cave so you can get some much-needed rest. Sleep peacefully knowing that the Russians you can see from your balcony can't hurt you anymore.

➤ OPTION #4

Embrace it. You've always said you wish there were more hours in the day; now there are. Get done all the things you've been putting off. After working around the clock on stuff you'll pass out eventually from exhaustion.

➤ OPTION #5

Blind yourself. Poke your eyes out and that way you won't see ANY light EVER. Sweet dreams.

IN THE FUTURE . . .

Develop a meth addiction. One hit of meth and the last thing you'll think about is sleep—you'll be too busy scrubbing your double-wide.

WTFACT: Most states have four seasons; Alaska also has four seasons: winter, still winter, almost winter, and construction.

WTFACT: Alaska state motto: North to the Future.

94. An Eskimo offers you his wife.

Forget Southern hospitality, no one knows how to make a visitor feel more at home than Eskimos. The Arctic may be a cold and unforgiving place, but the Eskimos know how to turn the heat up—especially for guests. Sure, the food may be better in the South (when was the last time you went out for Eskimo food?), but between grits and pussy, most of us would take pussy every day of the week and twice on Sunday. But while you appreciate the gesture, you really don't want to screw the Eskimo chick, despite the encouragement from her husband. Then again, you don't want to insult them. Hmm . . .

The WTF Approach to Turning Down a F*#!

> **OPTION #1**

Grin and fuck it. Eskimo pie anyone? Who the fuck do you think you are? What, you think that you are better than these people?

Who knows, she might be the best lover you've ever had. If not, she'll at least be the best Eskimo lover you've ever had.

➤ OPTION #2

Just say no. What's the Eskimo word for "hell no"? Tell the Eskimos you're married and that in your culture marriage is synonymous with monogamy—unless you're Newt Gingrich.

➤ OPTION #3

Fake it. Get this Eskimo and his wife shit faced, then when they wake up in the morning talk about how amazing the sex with his wife was. When they say they don't remember, act hurt and storm out. Problem solved.

WTFACT: In Canada and Greenland, the term "Eskimo" is considered pejorative. There are two major groups of indigenous peoples that "Eskimo" refers to: Inuit and Yupik. Aleut (as in the Aleutian Islands) is a third related group. Over 100,000 indigenous people live in Alaska out of a total population of about 700,000.

ESKIMOS ARE NO LAUGHING MATTER

- What do you call a gay Eskimo woman?
- A Klondike.

IN THE FUTURE . . .

Play gay. Tell him you're flattered but you never sleep with women.

95. Your Hawaiian vacation ends in a shark attack.

Your Hawaiian vacation was everything you dreamed it would be. Idle days spent on white sandy beaches, a piña colada in one hand and a favorite book in the other—all under a gentle blanket of endless sunshine. You saw volcanoes. You went snorkeling. You had oral sex with a stranger at a luau. Yes, it was the perfect vacation. Until that day you decided to take up surfing. Shark, meet vacationer; vacationer, meet shark. Yikes!

The WTF Approach to Surviving a F*#!-ing Shark Attack.

➤ STEP #1

Scream. As loud as you can. Scream as if the worst, most frightening thing is happening to you—because it is.

➤ STEP #2

Go for the eyes, gills, or snout. Playing dead is not going to deter an attacking shark. They're cleverer than they look. But, a swift kick or punch to the gills or the eyes might let the shark know that you mean business. So muster up all that Tae Bo you took last summer and beat the shit out of this fishy fuck.

➤ STEP #3

Negotiate. Make a deal with the shark, offering him fish for a year and a cameo in *When Sharks Attack*. Negotiate cautiously, though, he's a real shark when it comes to business.

➤ STEP #4

Pray. Of course, no one is listening, but you're running out of options at this point.

WTFACT: There are about sixty reports of shark attacks each year—all of which suck.

for the ladies . . .

Surfer Bethany Hamilton lost her arm in a shark attack then went on to become a professional surfer.

chapter thirteen

waiting to die in florida

96. You get married in Miami during hurricane season.

You've always wanted an outdoor wedding in the Sunshine State. Except you picked September, the middle of hurricane season. You were told the weather was going to be good on the big day, except right before the ceremony starts you see it. Dark skies, still air, it's the calm before the storm. You know in your gut things are about to go to shit, and you haven't even gotten married yet.

The WTF Approach to Making It Through the F*#!-ing Wedding Alive

➤ OPTION #1

Have a plan B. Make sure you have somewhere safe for you and your guests to run to when the hurricane hits. Then have a plan B for finding new family and friends, cause no one will want to talk to you after.

➤ OPTION #2

This is a sign. If a hurricane does hit on the day of your wedding, it's probably a sign that you are not supposed to get married, at least not to this bitch anyway. So when the storm passes tell your girl the wedding is off because God doesn't want you to get married. No one can argue with God.

Embrace it. How many people can say they got married in the middle of a hurricane? This definitely gives new meaning to "weathering the storm." Make T-shirts for you and your guests that say "We survived the Bergman-Miller wedding and all we got was this lousy T-shirt."

IN THE FUTURE . . .

Get married in Arizona; they have no weather there at all.

WTFACT: More storms hit Florida than any other U.S. state. We believe this is God's way of clearing out the white trash and the elderly.

WTF RANT

Why are hurricane names so lame? Hurricane Katrina, Hurricane Paul. These names make us believe that they're not so destructive. The names should inspire fear and destruction, like . . .

Hurricane Holy Shit!

Hurricane You Fucked up My Wedding!

Hurricane We're All Gonna Die!

WORST HURRICANE NAMES THROUGHOUT HISTORY

- FiFi
- Bob
- Earl
- Janet
- Hortense
- Beulah
- Mitch
- Opal
- Bieber (at least you know it's gonna suck, just by the name alone)

97. You live in Boca Raton and you're under the age of ninety.

You love living in Florida. The sun, the beach, the nightlife. Oh wait, you live in Boca Raton, where the night life starts at 5 P.M. and ends at 7 P.M. In a city swarming with wheelchairs you are the only one who doesn't consider an oxygen tank an accessory. Everywhere you turn it's gray hair, wrinkled faces, and the haunting laments of a life wasted. You're the only one who doesn't have one foot in the grave.

The WTF Approach to Living with Old People

> **OPTION #1**

Embrace it. Anywhere else in the world, you're a 4. But in Boca, you're a 10+. If you stay there, you will always be the "young" guy—until you hit your eighties, then you're just another old fart enjoying his golden years.

> **OPTION #2**

Marry a cougar. Not sure if they're called cougars at that age or saber-toothed tigers, but either way, find a rich old broad and sweep her off her walker. Marry her and wait for her to die, then take all the money and head to Miami and find yourself a hot young chick.

➤ **OPTION #3**

Start making babies. Start getting chicks pregnant and repopulate Boca with babies. Maybe the old people will get so annoyed with all the toddlers running around their once quiet city they will move to another city.

➤ **OPTION #4**

Open a funeral parlor. This is a no-brainer. These old fucks only have a few years to live, and when they die they're gonna have to go somewhere right? Open a funeral home and start raking in the cash. If you get really ambitious, open a cemetery as well; or if you have enough land, just bury them in your backyard.

WTFACT: Believe it or not, Florida is not the state with the oldest population in the United States. Maine is, with an average age over 42.

STATES WITH THE OLDEST POPULATIONS

1. Maine
2. Vermont
3. West Virginia
4. Florida

WTF RANT

Who says getting old is a bad thing? I can't wait to get old and really start living again. Truth is, seniors are a lot like college students. They sleep all day, watch TV, and piss their pants from time to time. I think they should open a senior living facility where you can drink, do drugs, and have unprotected sex (if you can still get it up). Who cares? You're 80; might as well go out with a bang and an STD.

WTFACT: According to several medical reposts, STDs have drastically increased among senior citizens. Because many seniors are now using drugs like Viagra they are more sexually active than before, and because they no longer fear pregnancy, they are not using protection, which has had a dramatic increase in STDs like syphilis and chlamydia. So listen up, old people and wrap that shit up.

CONDOM NAMES FOR MEN OVER SIXTY-FIVE

- Senior skins
- Trojan minimums
- Old bags

Florida's New Motto: FLORIDA: Relax . . . Retire . . . ReVote.

WTFACT: The literal translation of "Boca Raton" is "Mouth of the Mouse"

for the ladies . . .
Marry yourself a rich old fuck immediately.

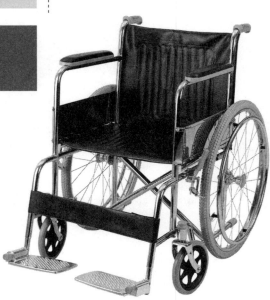

98. Your pet alligator breaks loose in your neighborhood.

It's a terrible feeling when a beloved pet goes missing. We've all been there. Will little Snuggles survive or will his little beagle body be smashed and flattened beyond recognition under the massive tires of a semi?

But when your favorite pet, Ally the Alligator, goes missing one day you have a worry of a different kind. Will he eat the newborn baby next door, or has he been too domesticated, his diet forever altered from fresh meat to the peanut butter and jelly sandwiches he's become accustomed to?

The WTF Approach to Finding Your F*#!-ing Pet

> **OPTION #1**

Bust out the PB & J. If that doesn't bring him running back home immediately, you might want to check on the baby next door.

> **OPTION #2**

Call animal control. There's got to be a number for missing alligators in Florida. You might get fined for keeping a flesh-eating killer as a pet, but as least you won't be charged with murder when Ally is caught ripping apart your neighbor.

> **OPTION #3**

Post some fliers. Put some pics up of Ally with her teeth fully exposed and tell people to be on the lookout. This will probably cause a citywide panic. No one will leave their homes, so you can have free range to find Ally.

WTF RANT

Taming the beast! Why do people own exotic animals as pets? They always seem to think they will be the one to "tame" them—it's like women who think they can change a man. One day your pet monkey rips your face off. Sure lion cubs are cute and cuddly, but guess what, moron, they grow up to be *lions*. Just look at what happened to Siegfried of Siegfried and Roy; his "tamed" tiger crunched down on his jugular and dragged him off stage. If a circus performer can't tame the wild beast, then no one can.

IN THE FUTURE . . .

Don't have an alligator as a pet, asshole. If you really like cold scaly pets, start with an iguana.

MATCH THE EXOTIC PET TO ITS WRATH

1. Chimpanzee

2. Cougar

3. Boa Constrictor

4. Shark

A. Biting your arm off

B. Biting off your face

C. Mauling

D. Suffocating

Answers: 1. B; 2. C; 3. D; 4. A

99. The East Coast "snowbirds" are taking over your Florida town.

Every year it's the same thing. From October until May, they come. They're big and loud and they are everywhere. They clog up the roads with shitty driving; crowd your favorite restaurants and complain about the service, even when it's good; and wipe out the small stores. They basically infest your sunny, warm town. And don't even get started about their annoying East Coast accents.

The WTF Approach to Surviving a F*#!-ing Snowbird Invasion

➤ OPTION #1

Exterminate them. That's what you do with annoying critters, right? Call up an "exterminator" and kill them all. That will teach those East Coast fucks to come to your town again.

➤ OPTION #2

Flip the switch. Go to their chilly East Coast town and take over. Bring your tan friends and start taking over their towns. Although they might not give a shit; to be honest, they might just be happy to have hot tan people to hook up with.

➤ OPTION #3

Close down the town. Get together with the other Floridians and decide to make your city very unwelcoming for these people. Start a strip club on every corner; bus in prostitutes and drug dealers. Soon these unwanted "visitors" will realize your little town is not the place they are looking for to relax, and soon they move on to another Florida town. You might want to keep one or two hookers just for fun!

WTFACT: The term *snowbirds* refers to retirees and business owners who have a second home in a warmer location, but Urban Dictionary has an even better definition: Irritating, disgusting old people, who come down to Florida from Northern states, drive like maniacs, and wear speedos on our beaches. God help us all. Sounds like we need a snowbird hunting season.

IN THE FUTURE . . .

Live somewhere where the elderly don't want to go, like Canada.

100. You're going to be late for the Early Bird Special.

It's getting late—it's almost 4 in the afternoon! You are going to be late for the Early Bird Special. Can you believe this woman? What the hell is taking her so long in the bathroom? Every week with this nonsense. What is she, nuts? No, truth is, she's just old and she can't move that fast. She really expects to show up and eat after the Early Bird Special? What kind of a person would show up after the Early Bird Special is over? It's unheard of. What to do when you're about to miss out on the special?!

The WTF Approach to Making It to an Early F*#!-ing Dinner on Time

➤ OPTION #1

Stay in. Forget it, there's always next week to meet up with all your retired friends. True, some will have inevitably passed away by that time, but that only means there will be fewer of you, making the early bird dinner far more intimate.

➤ OPTION #2

Splurge. Have dinner at regular prices and a regular time for a change. Don't worry about the money and have a great time. You only live once, remember. And for anyone living in Florida, that one time is coming to an end really, really soon.

➤ OPTION #3

Take charge. Pull your wife by the arm (careful, she could fall and break a hip), and get her in the car so you can make it to the Early Bird. Who cares if she is not done putting on makeup? And really, at her age does it even matter?

➤ OPTION #4

Go alone. If that old bag can't get her shit together, then leave and go get dinner without her. Take care of number one, you! If you want you can always get her something to go; that way you still save money and you look like the hero. Maybe your old lady will reward you later with a denture-free blow job. Now that's special!

101. You came to Florida to die but you just can't seem to.

>>>>> You planned on living out your golden years in the warm Florida sun. You're in the twilight of your life and all your affairs are in order. Your will is up to date, and you have said everything you need to say to your loved ones. You're as ready as you will ever be to leave this Godforsaken Earth. Except you won't die. Every time you think it's the end, you take a turn for the better. You even took up smoking again. Still, nothing. WTF? You've already outlived most of your friends and family; let's go already! You're 90+ and healthy as a horse. Damn, what it's gonna take to die?

The WTF Approach to Moving On Already

➤ OPTION #1

Take matters into your own hands. Extreme, we know, but shit, if you really want to "go," then go already. Of course some believe you won't get into heaven if you do, so make it look like an accident. Start acting like you're losing your mind, then one night polish off a bottle of sleeping pills. No one will believe that at your age you purposely offed yourself. Then again, with your luck someone will find you and save your old decrepit ass. On second thought, driving off a bridge gives you better odds of getting the job done.

➤ OPTION #2

Live hard. Maybe that's why you've lived so long, cause you've been playing it safe. Well enough! Start drinking, doing drugs, riding on motorcycles. You might just have some fun before your heart gives out.

➤ OPTION #3

Live forever. Maybe you're a vampire or some other trendy immortal. Try shifting your focus from dying to living—you might like it.

➤ OPTION #4

Move somewhere else. Maybe there's something in that Florida water that keeps you from dying. Go to Alaska and see how long your old ass survives.

OH HOW WE'VE GROWN: AVERAGE LIFE EXPECTANCY THROUGH THE YEARS

- 1850: 38 years
- 1930: 59 years
- 1960: 67 years
- 1980: 70 years
- 1995: 73 years
- 2001: 75 years
- 2012: 81 years
- If you're famous, however, your expectancy is 27 years

WTFACT: The official world record for the oldest person is Jeanne Calment of France, who lived to be 122 years and 164 days old. That's probably because the French are so mean; she just refused to die.